HEALING DUST
poems of survival

Florinda Ruiz

Solis Press

Photographic credits: all photographs © Florinda Ruiz, except for page 8; page 30; page 38; page 40 Metropolitan Museum of Art, New York; page 42 Freepik

Cover: photograph of the author by Mark Rush

Published in 2025 by Solis Press

ISBN: 978-1-910146-94-1

Published by Solis Press, England

Web: www.solispress.com | *X/Twitter*: @SolisPress

Contents

Florinda Ruiz, 1961–2024

FLORINDA RUIZ was born on 12 November 1961 in Guadalajara, Spain. She received her B.A. in classical languages at the Universidad Autonoma de Madrid and an M.A. and Ph.D. in classical languages from Johns Hopkins University. She taught Spanish and Classics at Washington and Lee University before moving on to the Department of Foreign Languages at Roanoke College, where she retired as associate professor in 2007. She was honored with the Dean's Exemplary Teaching Award in 2005–6. She finished her academic career at Washington and Lee University where she served as director of the Writing Program from 2014 to 2023.

Florinda published across a variety of disciplines. Her essay "Why I Write About War" appeared in the collection *Collateral Damage* (University of Virginia Press, 2021) edited by Bárbara Mujica. Her "Human Cries Keep Falling Like Summer Rain" appeared in *Voices on the Move* edited by Domnica Radulescu and Roxana Cazan (Solis Press, 2020). With her colleague, Gary Gibbs (Roanoke College), she co-authored several pieces on Arthur Golding's work on Ovid's *Metamorphosis*. She was also the voice of Rosetta Stone's Spanish courses in 2007 and 2010.

Florinda was an avid poet and award-winning photographer. After her cancer diagnosis, she dedicated herself to sharing her poetry and photos with the community of cancer patients around the world. To that end, she assembled this volume in hopes of offering comfort and healing to others. She is survived by her husband of 36 years, Mark Rush; sons William and Alex; daughter-in-law, Meaghann; granddaughter Celia; mother Florinda; brother Guillermo; and a pup, Humphrey that still looks after her husband.

Prologue

We walk through our overscheduled lives in a rush, taking care of those around us, our work, our obligations, often forgetting to take care of ourselves. Then, suddenly, a ghostly intruder makes its own space in our life and becomes part of it. By the time we truly notice the full weight of its presence, this "thing" is here to stay. There is no escaping it, no ignoring, we must face it. It rests like an encroacher in the middle of our being, our family, our health, our home, our relationships, our mind, our work, and it grows stealthily in gradual advances giving birth to sprawling fears, doubts, distress. It wakes up with us every morning and often disturbs our sleep at night. We just can't stay the course as it is, one must do something, say something, create something, for sure change something. Where and how to start?

It is clear this "thing" is focused on us. We must address its effect on ourselves to prevent it from affecting those around us. No matter our past, we must find time: time to reflect, change and learn, unlearn, or relearn. It is time for transformation, for new pathways, new tools, new thinking patterns, new strategies. Sometimes, a loved one will guide us through a new doorway, sometimes we find a dedicated professional we can connect with, a wise book with a new vision, or an unexpected inspiration from a total stranger. But the most important tool to move forward and confront such kind of intruder is in our own soul. It is the soul that provides the keys to unleash the spirit and determination we need for action. I believe I already possess the ability to unravel the threads of my emotions, to comb away any worthless knots, to examine the little details of a particular experience, to bravely name their parts, and draw their elements. The knowledge I need to understand my feelings and how a new situation might affect my world is within me. Once we identify and confirm that we are under siege, the key to rescue the self begins with a decision to listen to ourselves with kindness, to pay attention to the details of our story as if a dear friend were telling it to us. When we tend to a friend in trouble, we do so carefully, respecting their feelings, creating an environment of trust and tranquility that will help revitalize a broken spirit. We must do the same for *our own* broken soul. Our wounds will heal surrounded by warmth, care, trust, and acceptance. It is time for our mind to take action, time to build and adopt new habits that won't be forgotten, new paths for survival.

I made the decision to become my best companion, to treat my soul the way I would treat that dear friend in need of comfort, peace, and joy. What does she need? I'd ask. No matter what type of intruder you have, you can build for your dear self the agency and courage to confront it. The "it" could be an actual person, a piece of information, a newly found truth or a lie, an illness, an action, a forgotten memory. My intruder is an illness that is here to stay. One who, uninvited and stealthy, snuck in while I was happily paying attention to life. Initially, I went throughout a sorrowful list of unanswerable questions – "why me?", "how can this be?", "am I dreaming?" "what did I do wrong?'– followed by long bouts of intense tearful sadness over the grief that this intruder was spreading through my surroundings, my mind, my family, my present, and my future. One night, I saw myself there, in the corner of a blue room, numb, insecure, confused, scared of my changed future, fearful of the endless uncertainties amassing round of me, and decided to take action. An intruder can quickly alter our sense of reality. Ideas we've entertained for years now crumble, making us suffer, forcing us to consider the imperfections of our dreamed futures, their feeble nature. We can only build on the present, not our past – solid ground, not sand. We must let go, even if it threatens desires and habits we mistakenly convinced ourselves were vital to our being: in my case, the hopes and dreams for my elderly years. I realized I needed to eliminate useless longings for what cannot be. I am accountable to the version of the self I am right now. This present self now has invited me to discover its beauty and potential, the faint flame of hope flickering feebly in the storm, yet remaining lit.

I named and charted the feelings and emotions that my storm brought, one poem at a time. I knew that a renewed vision of the future would save me from sinking in the fear of losing myself, of losing the old me. My mind generated alternative images and hopeful future experiences to erase any negative energy. As I looked back, throughout all my years, I saw how I had already transformed and adapted numerous times. My task now was to rechart a personal map, open a path to follow that also included the courage from my most heartbreaking life moments, the essential strength I extracted from them and the healing power dust that still lives in my core. The practice of reconstructing my grit, of restoring visions of hope and new experiences with words, images, and color has always given me comfort, spirit, and resilience during hard times. I couldn't let myself face any new experiences or emotions alone, without support, without new tools, without my caring company, without a smile, without a vision for a positive outcome, without a realistic wish to move forward. It takes discipline, self-awareness, and dedicated agency. My new poetic re-drawings are rearticulations of thought patterns and hopes. The goal is to leave the fragile scaffolding that barely keeps us standing and find our way back to a sense of solid self, a more complete and resilient persona.

Indeed, grief can come anytime as a deluge that floods into us and saturates it all like a swamp, like quicksand. It can make our spirit soggy and heavy and we feel untethered and adrift. This is because grief always implies a loss, the loss of one's own prior view of the future, of our life's former expectations, of the world we thought we had created for ourselves. Grieving has its own plans, inhabiting forgotten corners of our minds, so we must examine any neglected spaces and let grief move into a refurbished alcove in our lives, a serene and joyful place without anxiety. I have discovered the intruder's capacity to add certain joys of its own, its agency to trigger gratitude for my entire life, its power to deliver as much anguish and grief as it could calm and serenity. I realized I could attempt to befriend it without fear and even tame it. I learned that joy expands our thinking and fills us with a new and intense appreciation for life. It allows us to create new visions that bring contentment, tranquility, peace, satisfaction, "enoughness", gratitude, and comfort. And so we learn to be kind to our quivers, to the shudder of vulnerability that inevitably attacks our spirit at times. On those occasions, we need to summon and call joy forth, intentionally, to manifest itself and live within us firmly, to be ready to create solid environments and restorative moments. Joy fuels hope.

And so the visions of this book occurred: sorrow overhauled by a breeze of sparkling healing dust. My intruder has found its serene place and its experiences are transformed without hiding its fears. We can sit together at the bottom of our own glass snowball and quietly observe the beauty that still surrounds us, all the little wonders that shower us if we shake our world gently. We can't remove suffering, but we can transform it. To get there we need to allow new hopes to be born by letting joy caress our grief as it speaks openly about the bitterness, anger, self-blame, remorse, or regrets we have built. We must commit ourselves to become gardeners of the spirit – tending and turning the soil of our soul, and allowing the light of our mind to bring new growths and pathways.

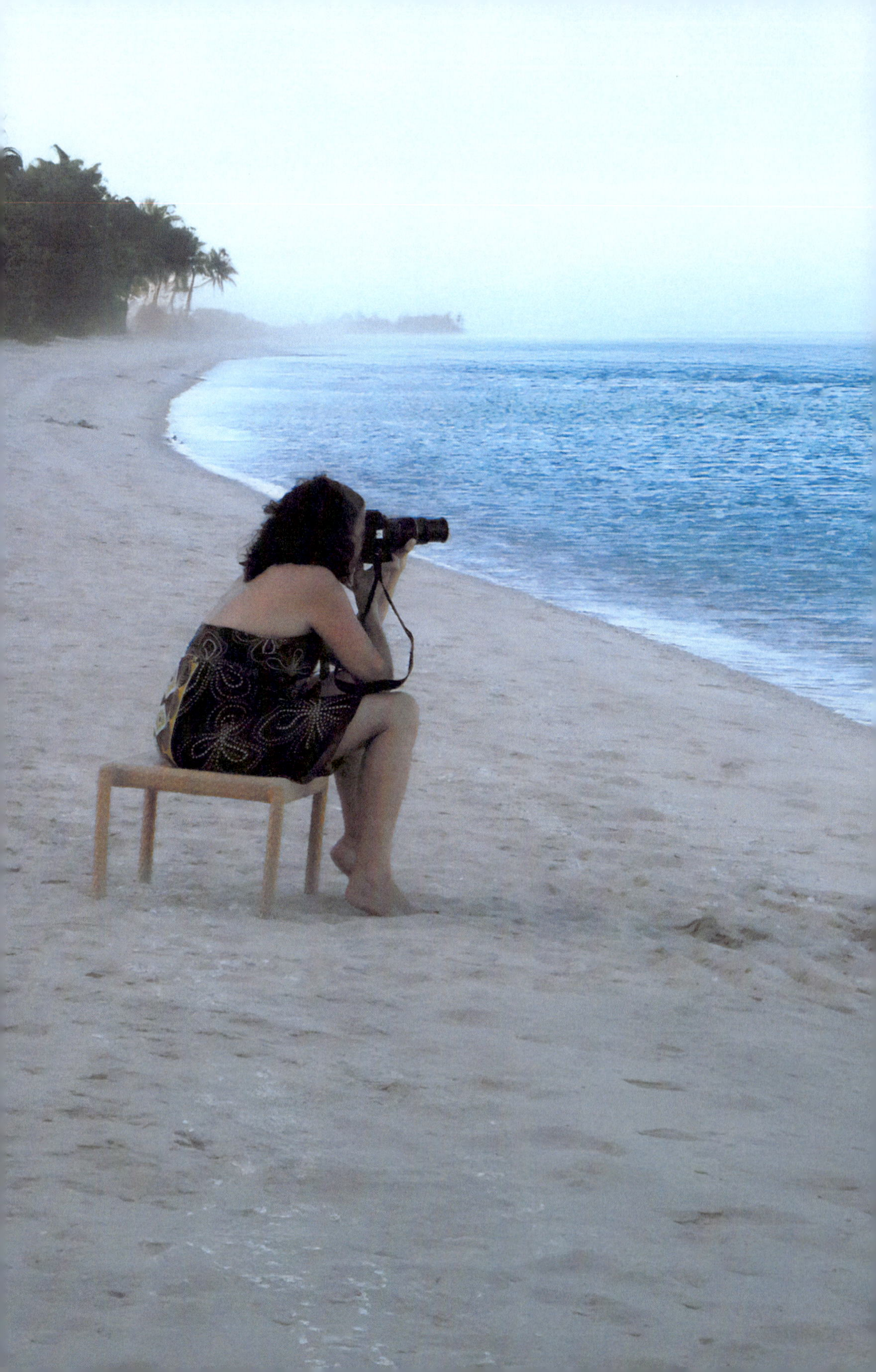

1 Birthday Surprise Film

The sun plunged swiftly
into the depth of my mountains.
A confused morning sunset
filled an unbecoming day,
unrevised storyboard page,
unapproved closing frame,
unexpected live film finale.

Who oversaw that shooting?
The camera rolled on
off-cue
off-beat
following an odd script
in ominous dénouement,
the culmination of an awry plot
with no director in sight.

Essential shifts press on now:
reassemble the production team,
review the footage,
retake those scenes,
rearrange the sequences,
rebuild the outcome.

The enormity of that day
mustn't attain a tragic tinge;
its transcendence must shine,
its vastness transform the future,
its magnitude illuminate my soul,
its bearing emblazon a metamorphosis.

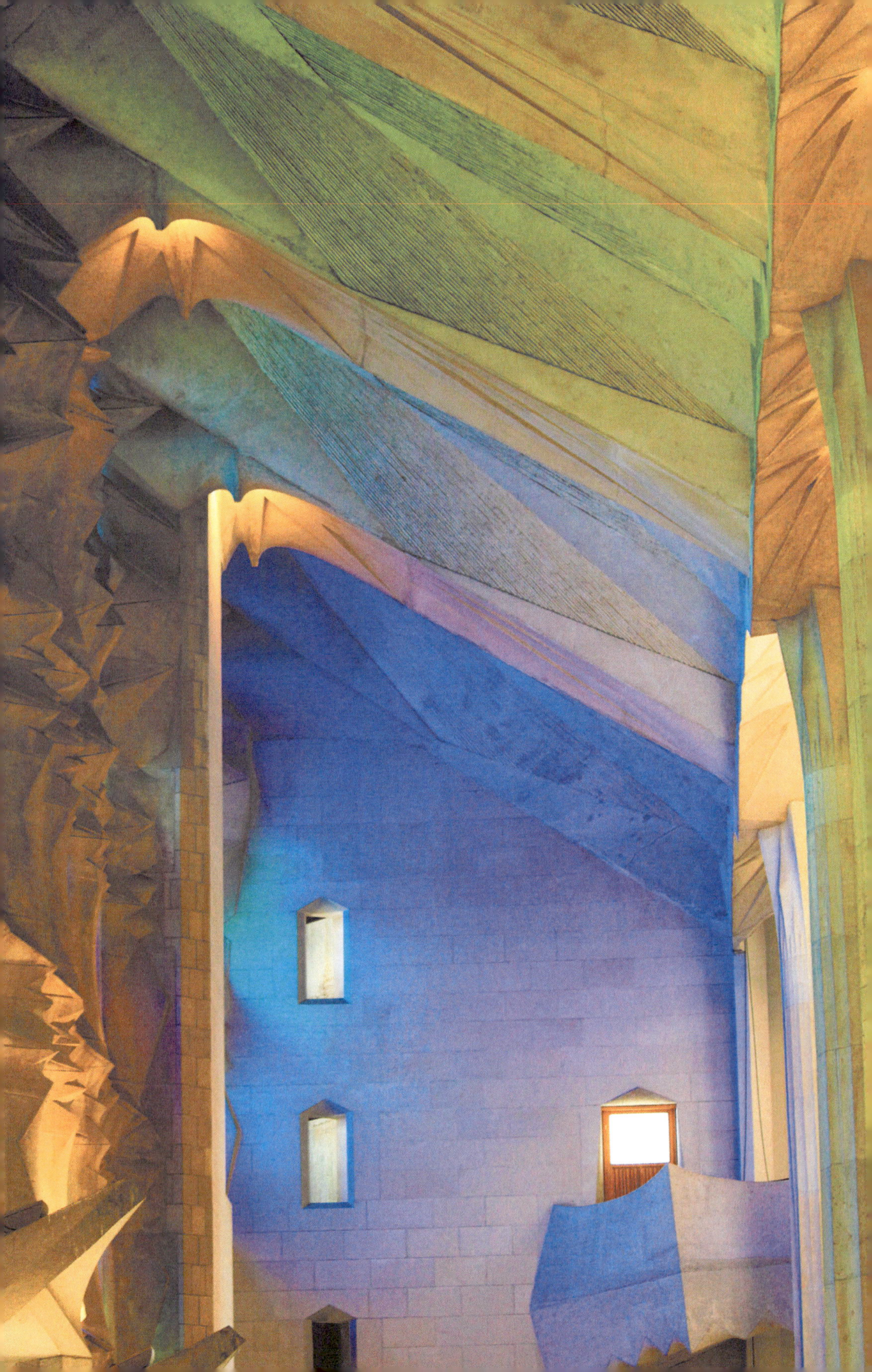

2 The C-Word

The word strikes and
a blow to life ensues
rushing against columns of strength,
eroding my building's main fixtures,
yet without enough cracks to topple it.

One motif hums now through each day
with unbearable nagging suspicions.
The future tries to hijack the present
and serenity begins to frail
while dust seeps through new fissures,
while blazing fears burst into new ashes,
while fright permeates new crevices
and gray follows gray under the storm.

A talisman must ward off this intruder
and soak its embers in hope,
must transform this shack
into a rock-solid sacred sanctuary
that thwarts any smoldering debris.

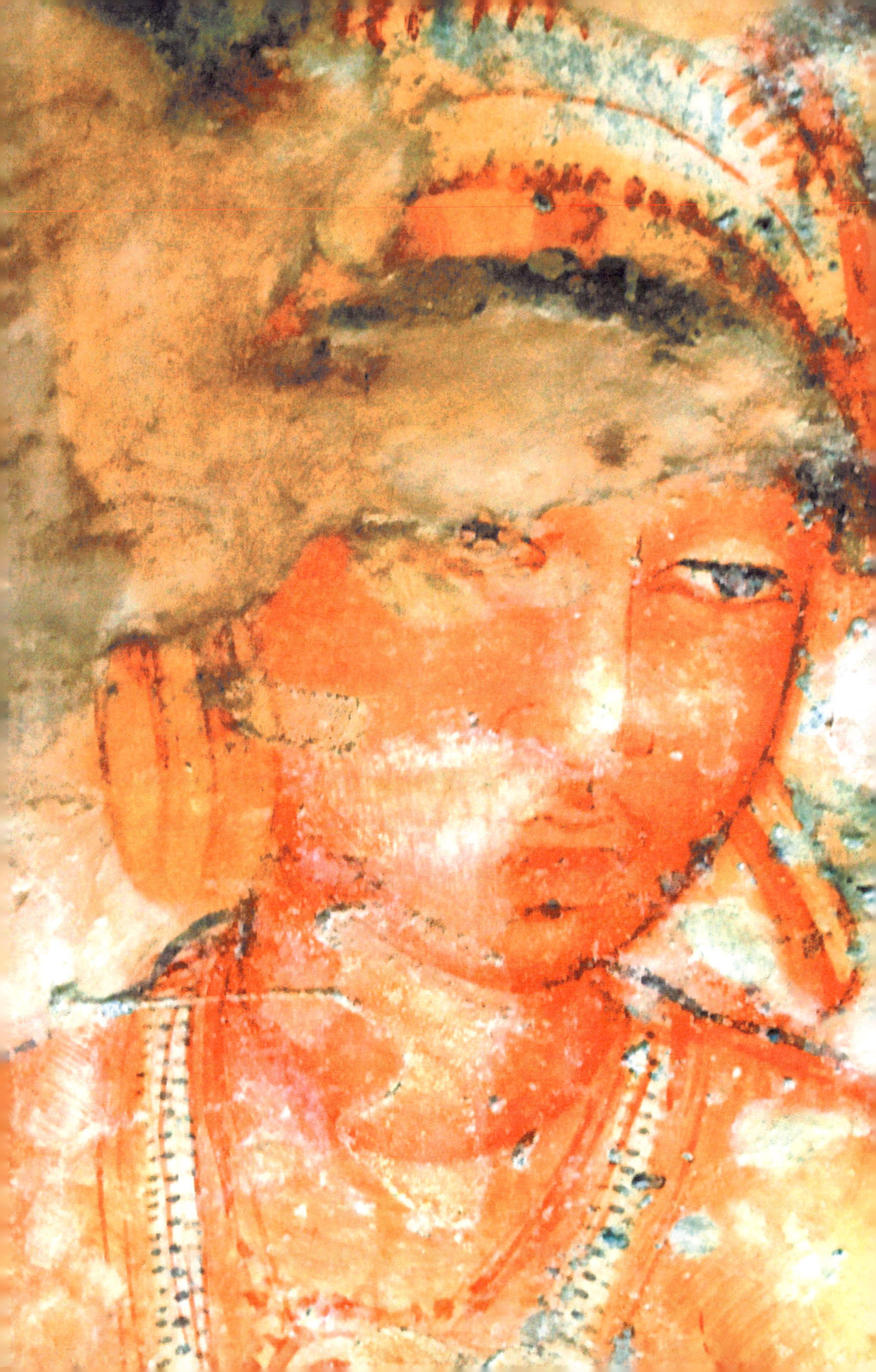

3 Other People

I've become the other people,
the sort who endured
what I face now,
nice people with rough lives
and pip cards instead of aces,
omitted in the plot line
of a dreamed reality,
missing from the easy flow
of my lucky star of yore.

I am those others now
dealt with the overlooked
hazards of their decks.
I play their implacable lots,
their shuffle, my new story,
far from what I mapped out,
close to what wouldn't come,
close to what only happened
in other people's lives.

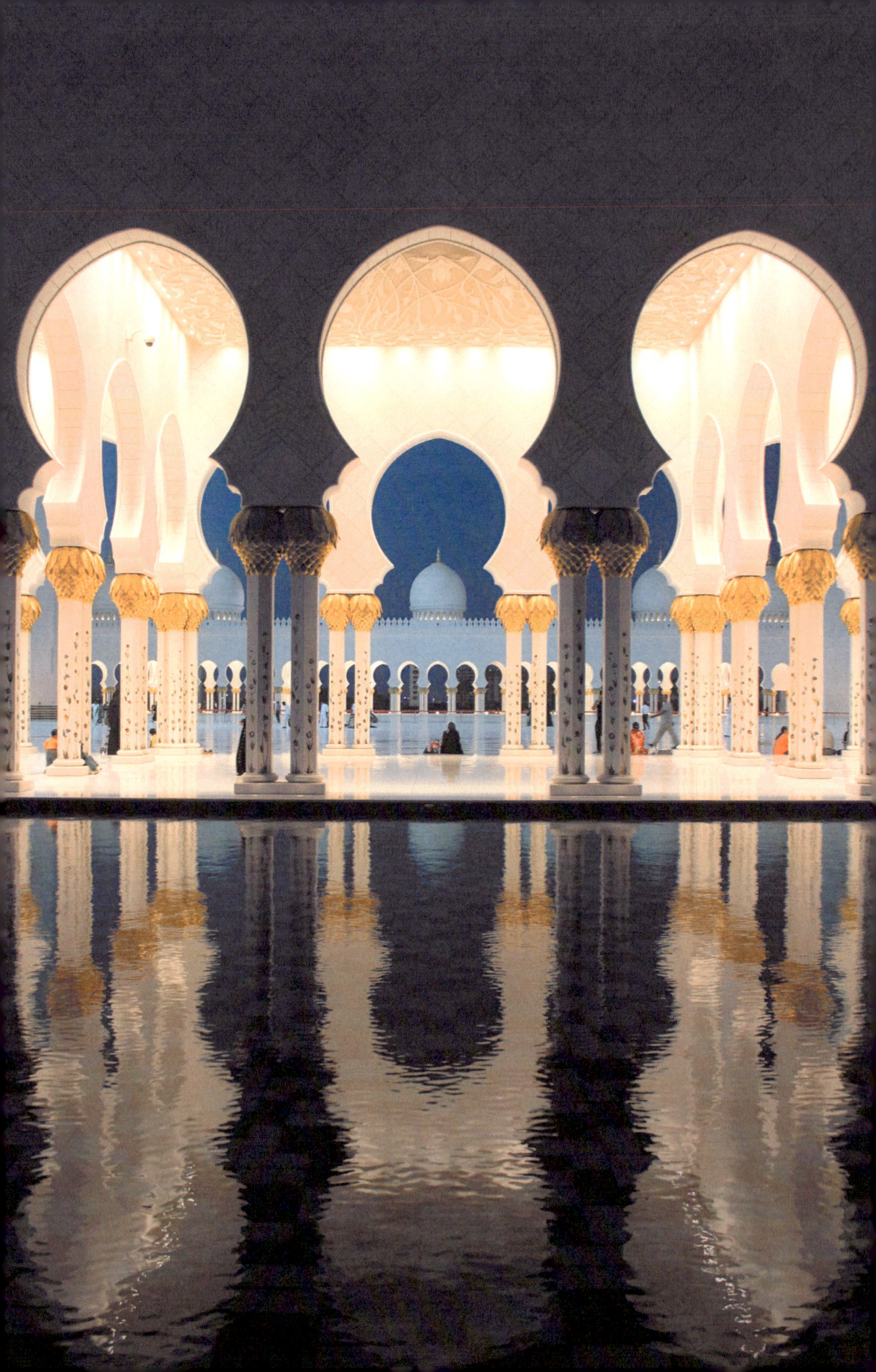

4 A Spell For Renewal

Isis, Sirona, Eir, Aja,
inhale the ashes of my brazier.
Scatter the ambers into the four winds.
Never to return.
To be no more.
The north to replace them with health.
The east to replace them with strength.
The south to replace them with light.
The west to replace them with life.

Cast a healing circle.
Draw down the moon.
Wrap the embrace of its light
over my tangled throat.

Hold a blessing chalice.
Spread the anointing oil.
Paint the power of its scent
over my shaking limbs.

Light a white virgin candle.
Brighten this bleak altar.
Unfurl the glow of its flame
over my shaded thoughts.

Smudge my shrine with sage.
Scatter sweetgrass on all corners.
Infuse the energy of its aroma
over the rhythms of my breath.

Awaken new dancing spirits.
Tap the hide of a joyful drum.
Harmonize the voices of its beating
over my heart's faint vibrations.

Unfold layers of gold leaf.
Sprinkle the healing dust.
Gild the shine of its aura
over my charred radiance.

May the thunder of your spirits
dispel the fury of this ruthless foe,
untrap the zeal of my mind,
and release the fire of my being.

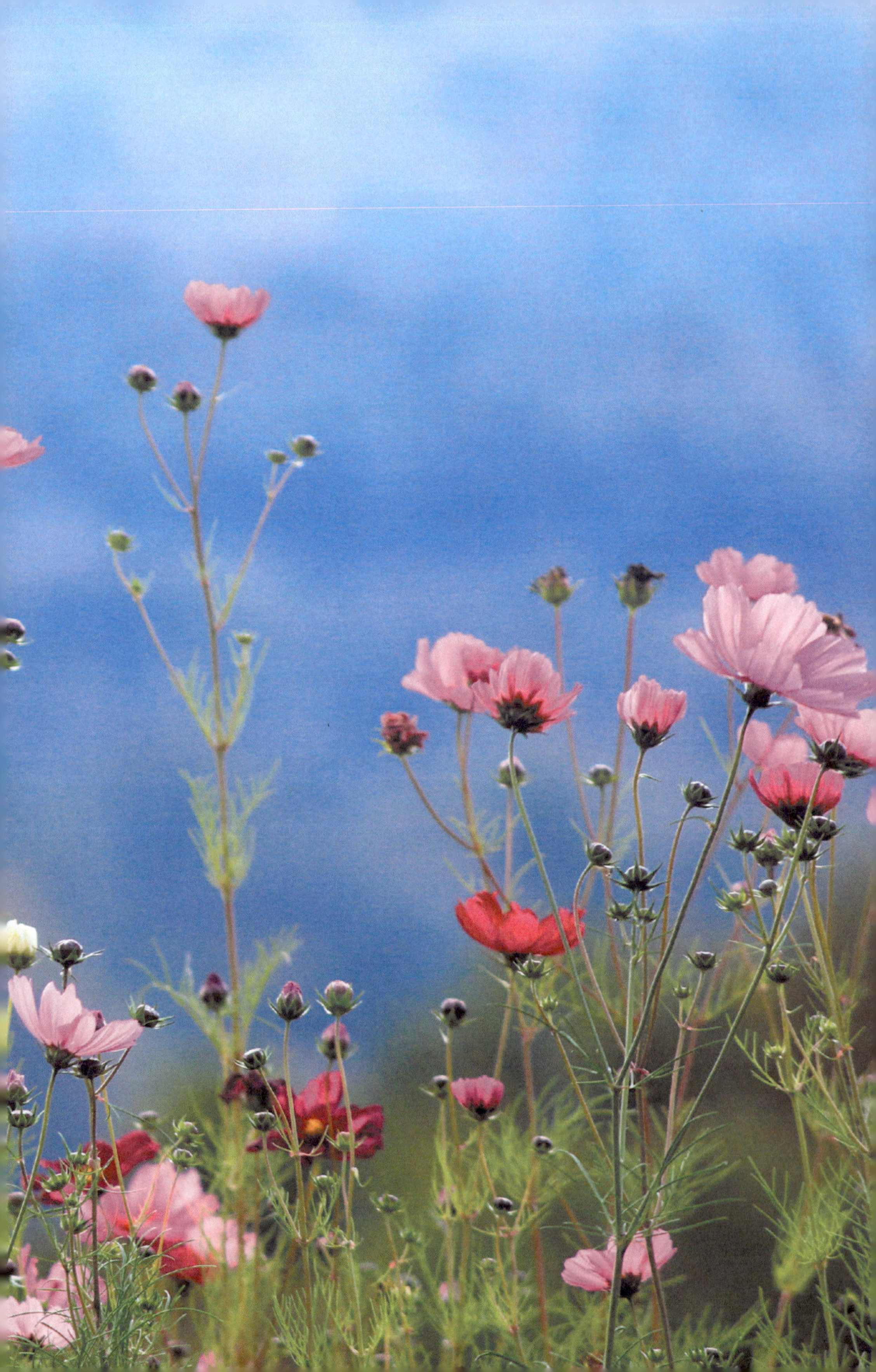

5 Garden Upkeep

The mind is girded for the fray,
for the angst and panic invasion.
It strays
in and out of kudzu fears
like a sprawling myrtle,
a pretty creeper periwinkle
of indolent trailing stems.

Its vigorous leafy growth,
its noxious hardy roots
try to ambush my garden,
disrupt the harmony in my head,
and crowd the stillness in my brain.

I'll pluck each secret terror,
the myriad fretful vines
lest they cloak and bury my spirit.

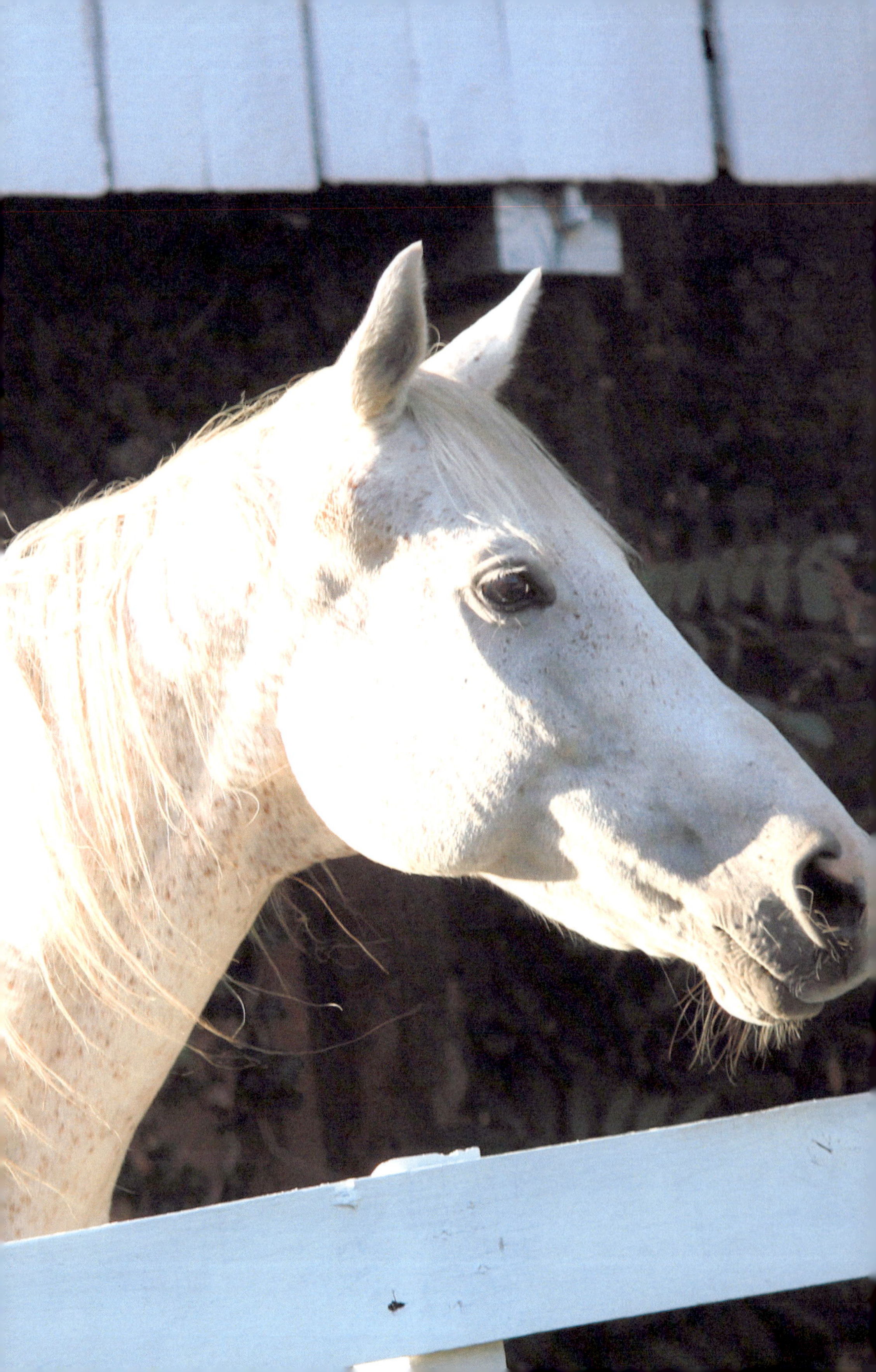

6 It Was Frestón's Fault

I charged at full speed
but his sails didn't halt.
In a swing within twirl
his ferocious giant's arms
hurled me, like a snowflake,
out of the dancing loop,
tossed in a field of windmills,
holding my nameless lance,
frozen and horseless,
pulled away from *Rocinante.*

Still sane, just disheveled.
Only a sorcerer's initial advantage
before my plan to defeat him is set.

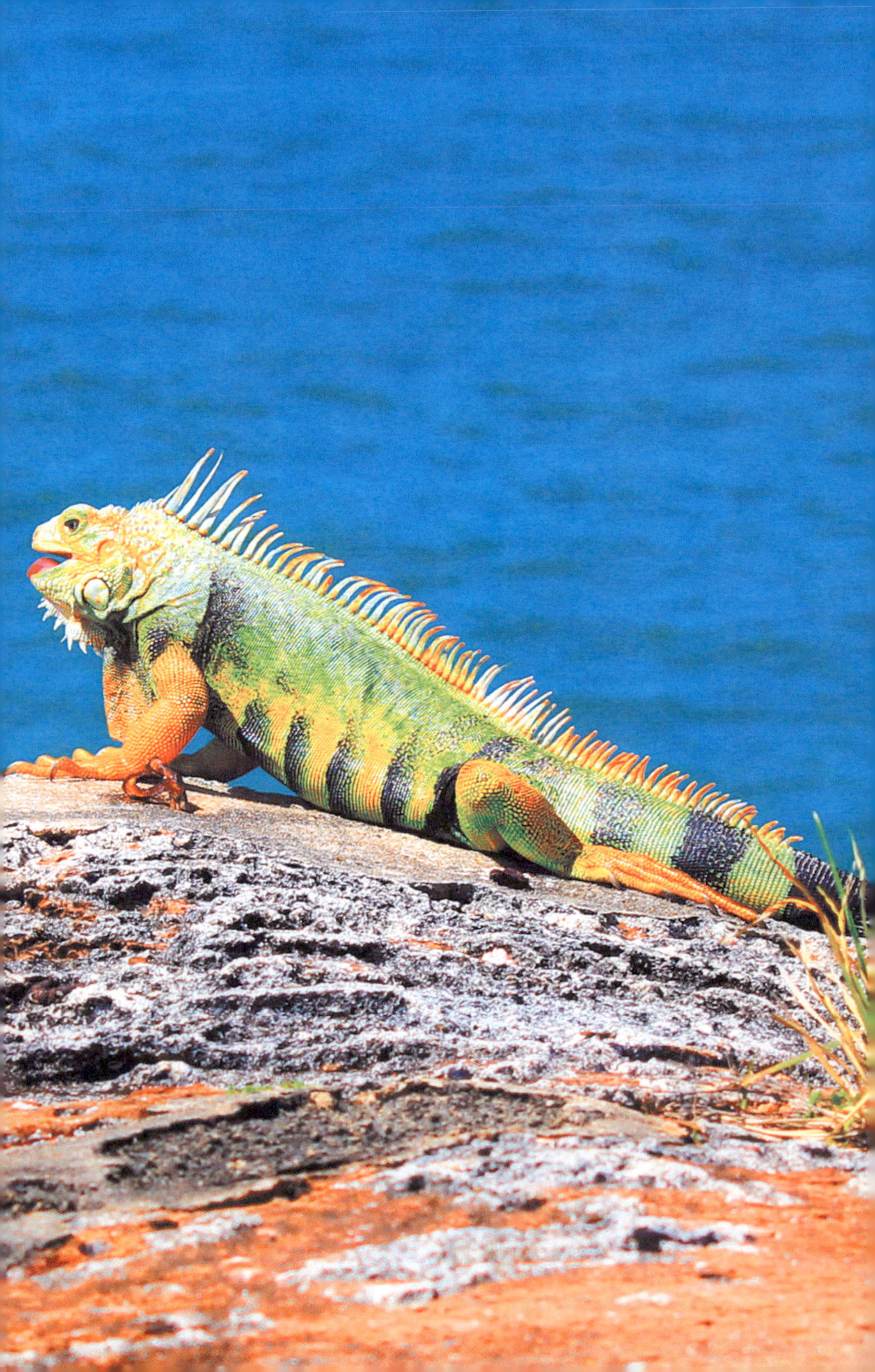

7 Healing Hunt

On the prowl for a bite of life,
she's a bruised brave animal
soaked in a dreaminess of being,
eyes fixed only on survival.

She has shed all sorrow and salt
out of her jabbing dire tears,
muster a stricken smile,
not a trace of gloom or fear.

A chilling veil of deep gray haze,
can't shield her spark and cheer,
nor transform fright into fate
at each daunting new frontier.

Pushing along with brisk steps,
she knows to keep an even pace
to hunt the forces of healing,
to hoard serenity into her mace.

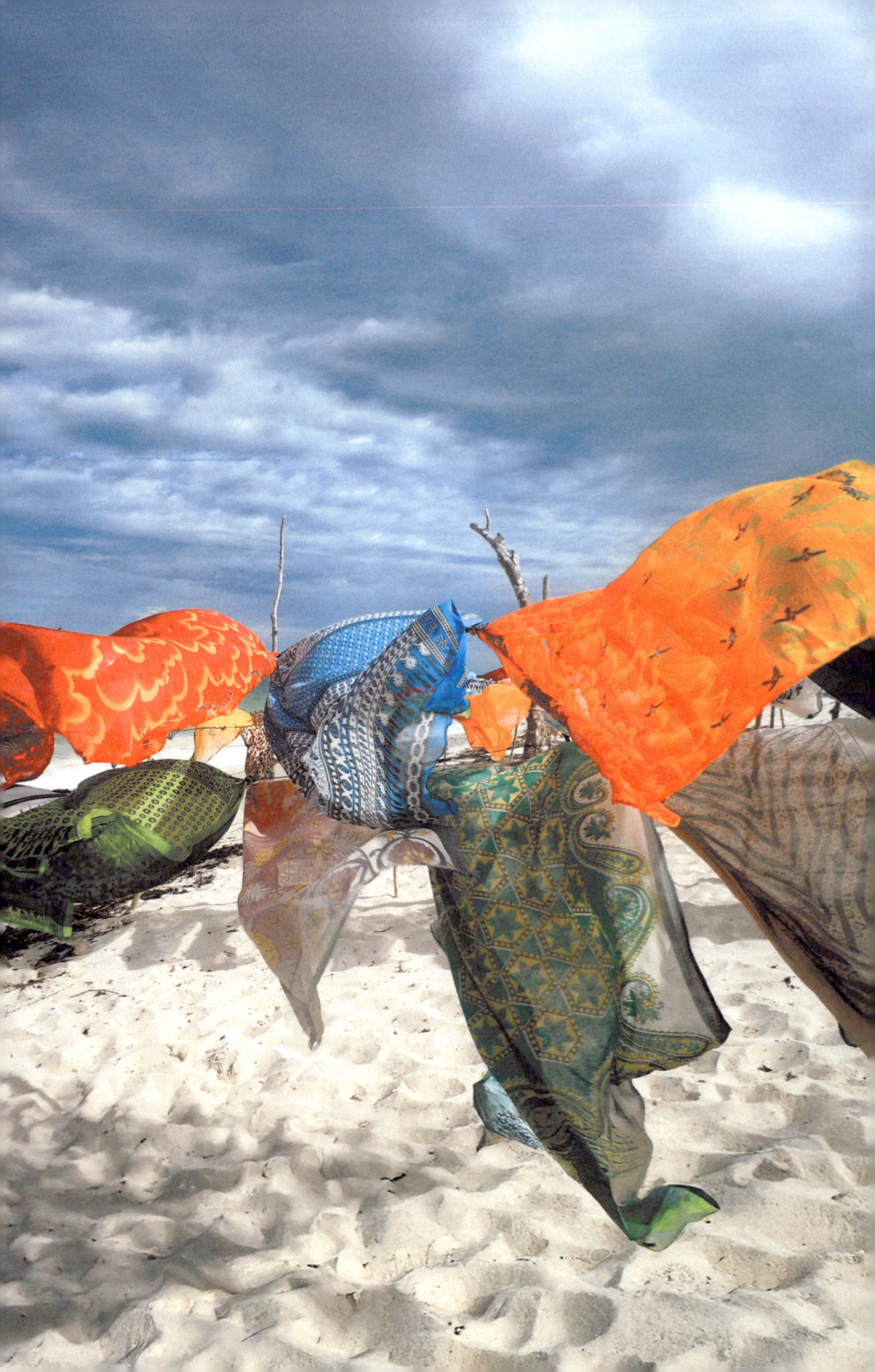

8 In My Power

I must erase your worries
in order to save myself.
I can't unlace a blush of fright
cuz my words mold your cool
and your growing calm
builds my fortitude back.

I gotta build your strength
with a brimful of my hopes,
cheerful veils over my grief,
cuz my joy dispels your sorrow
and your moments of respite
maintain my mind's solace.

9 From Earth to Soul

A universe wheel spin can re-cast us into corporeal earthlings
and turn our essence into a howling telluric magnetic field.

I'm not armed with a bright radioactive roar.
Although I'd like to bid this invader disappear,
I'd rather whoosh all energy to the soul's kernel,
listen for its quiet echoes,
redeem the days left to this existence.
No baleful thoughts, no dreary wails,
no eroding regrets, no desperate fights,
no sharp griefs, no scratchy dirges,
just becoming instrument to a gentle melody
without piercing strings of sorrow,
without remains of broken frets of hope,
without the pungent woes of a bow arched in distress,
only the airy fluting that accompanies a serene passing.

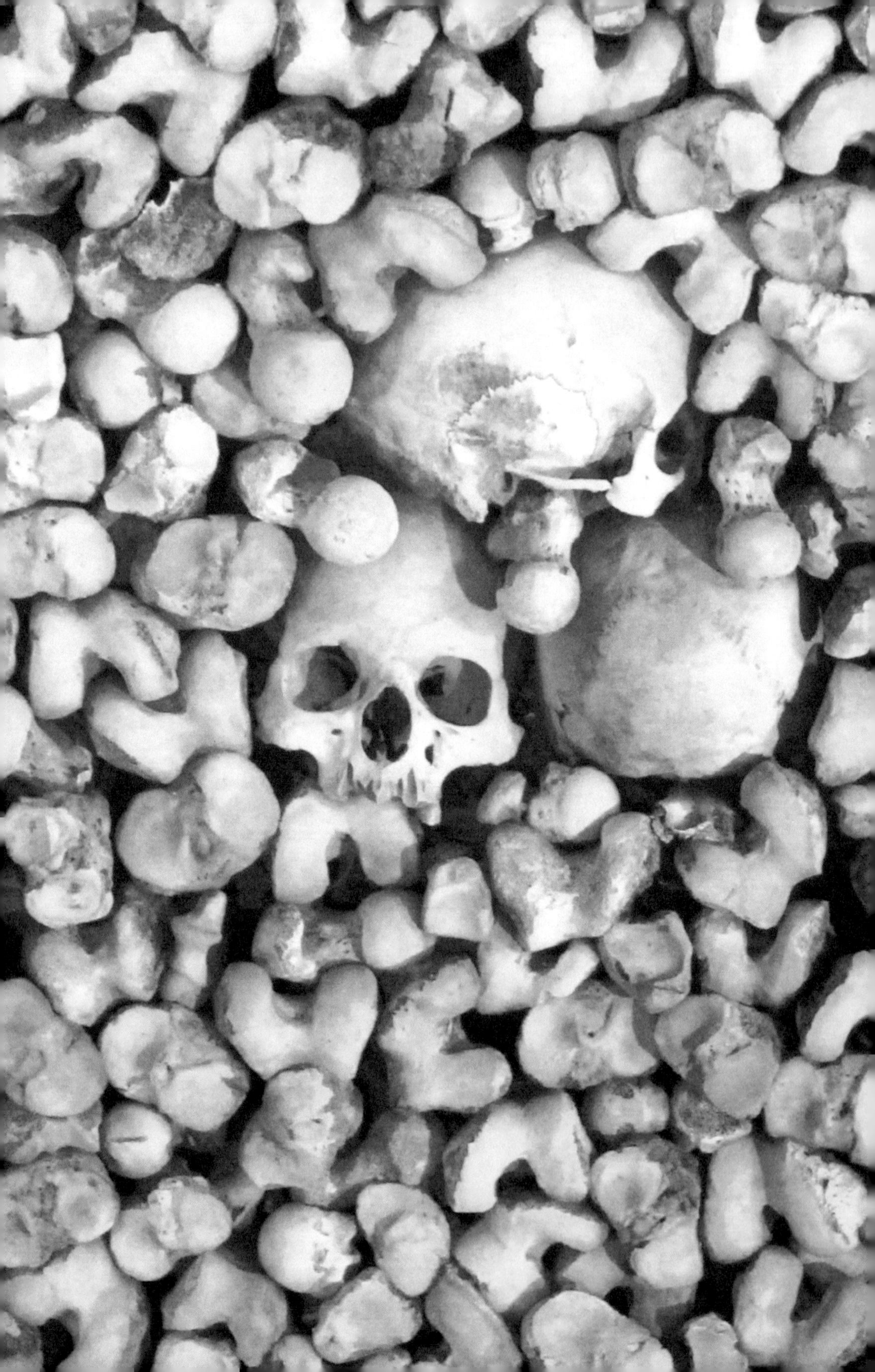

10 The Pill

Hard work ahead,
little golden jewel.
Don your charm,
beam your sparkle,
wave your wand,
whirl your magic
without faint heart.
Triumphant
may you reign
in this altar of ours.

Our engagement gem,
Our daily ceremony,
Our extended journey,
Our love and laughter,
Our vows of hope,
Our commitment is courage,
Our pledge, perseverance,
Our pact, purpose,
Our power, patience
Our secret, serenity.

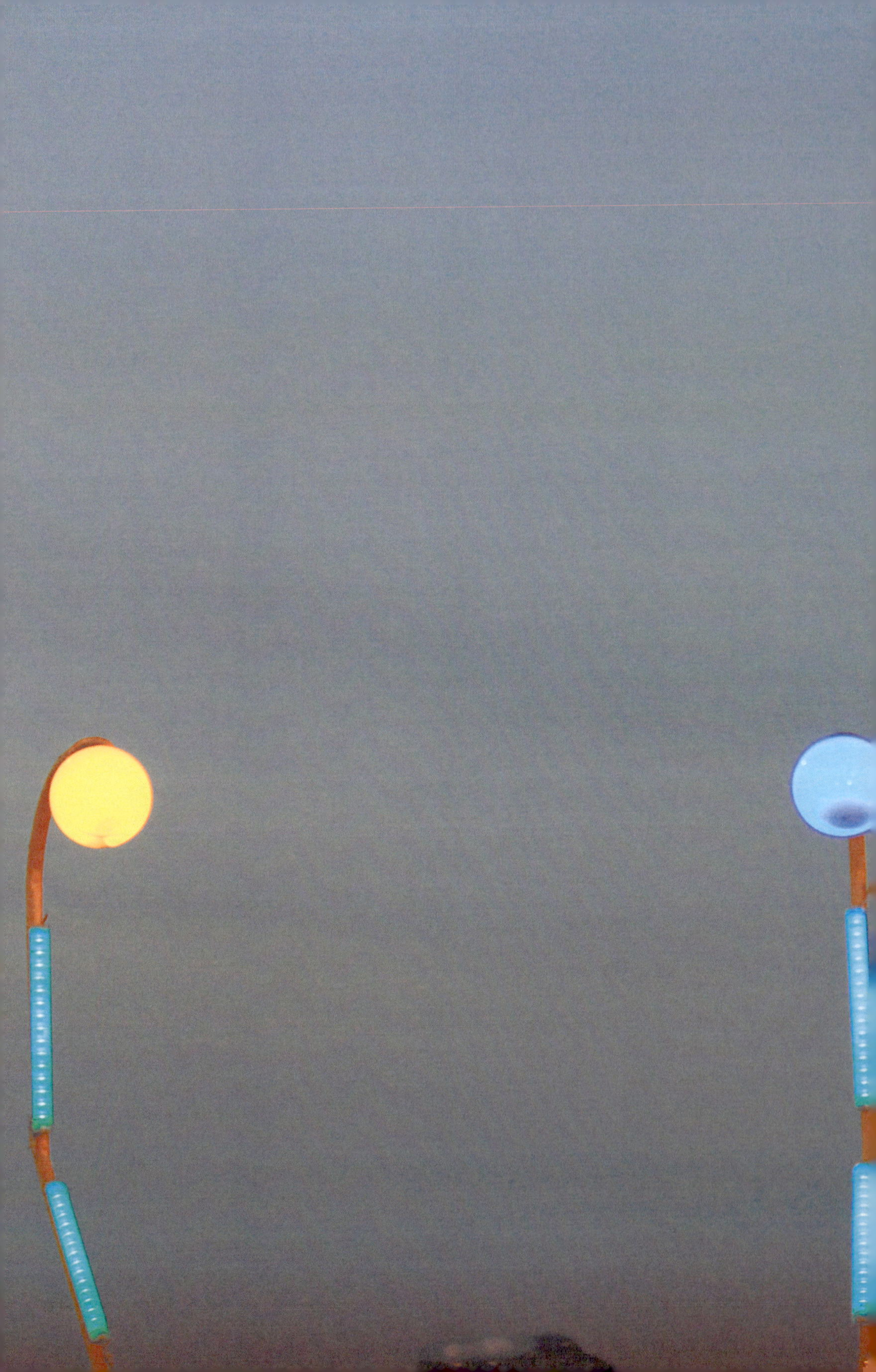

11 Radiation Station

Trapped in space under the sun of radiation,
I'm surrounded by three connected satellites,
orbiting:
one big round tub,
one chunky square,
one flat shiny screen.
What's inside the round metal tub?
Might the heavy silver cube fall?
Why is the cold screen imageless?
A green neon-like bright beam seeps through,
scouts the space with linear cosmic quietness,
moving over my tattooed-body's guiding points,
still frozen under the warm comfort blanket,
ready for the magic of silent cool burning.

Thirty flowery branches of a red-bud tree
pick faithfully down at my new universe
from a bright happy fake ceiling window,
an opening of light and hope filled sky,
reminder of the world beyond radiation station.

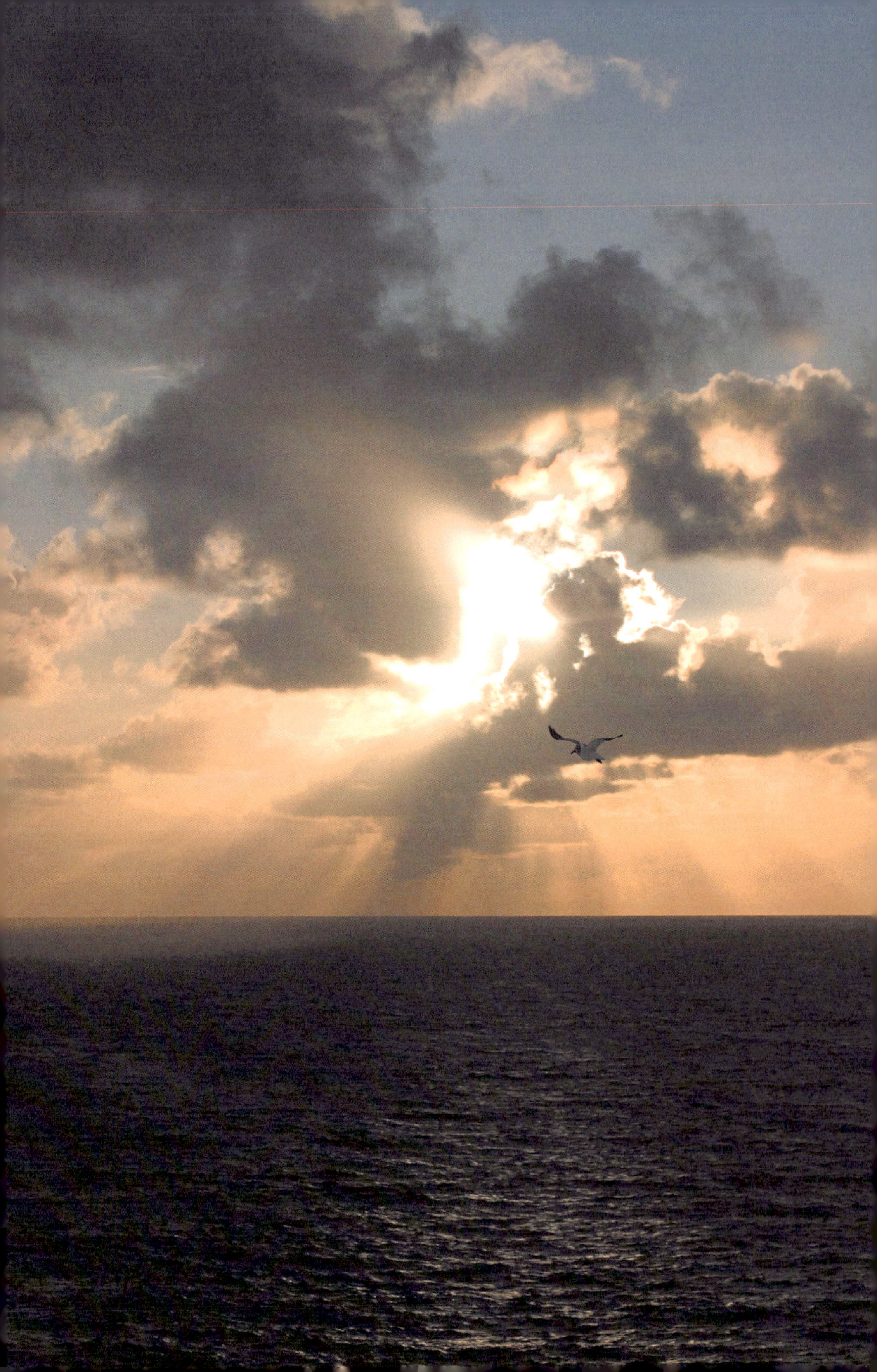

12 Close

Close
to drinking the pure nectar
of our infinite universe.
Close
to touching the stars
in the cosmos' vast fullness.
Close
to finding the fluid secrets
of the ocean's hidden depths.
Close
to joining the majesty of nature
with my life's little drop.
Close
to lighting the candle
where new hearts' flames live.
Close
to holding the wisdom key
that unties life's knots.
Close
to unfolding the entirety
of the rest of my soul.
Close
to embracing the inner bond
of every parcel of my being.
Close
to admiring the soulful sprouts
from all of my lives' seeds.
Close
to hearing the cherished voices
from past and present journeys.
Close
to becoming the nightly breeze
that swirls with a full moon's music.
Close

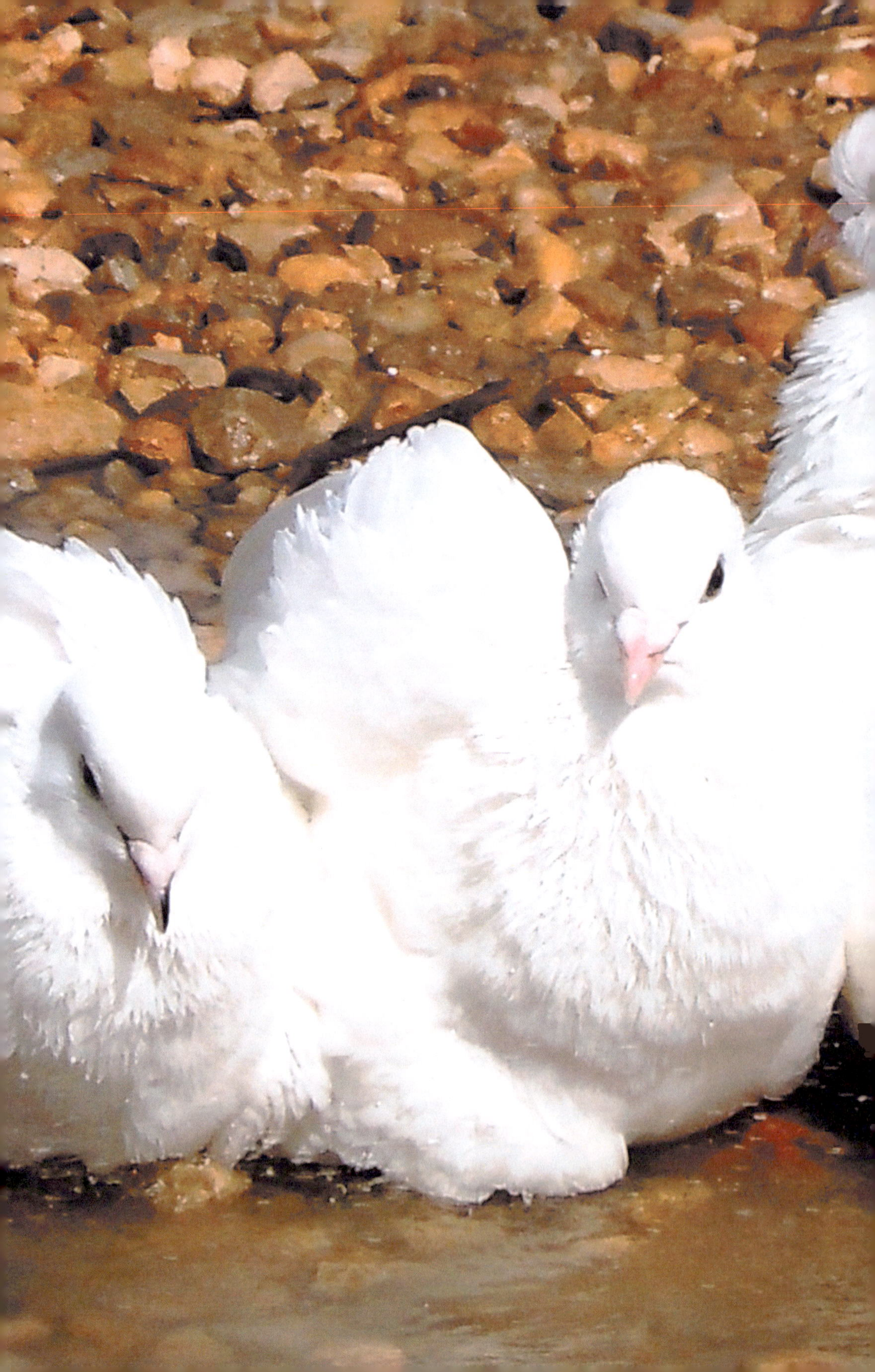

13 The Dove Flock

When Goddess Ishtar emerged
as a giant dove
from a central palm tree
in the garden temple of Aššur,
near her ancient Mesopotamian Uruk,
a solemn dovecote was formed,
a coven treasury of holy souls,
a sacred columbarium of enchanted chirps.

Each '*peristera*', περιστερά,
claimed the Greeks,
was a pigeon bird of Ishtar.
Sacred beings to Aphrodite,
messengers of good spirit,
soothers of worried, troubled thoughts,
pathfinders of renewal in the silence of the mind,
harbingers to inner peace, calm, and purpose.

Our Gray Dove flock, a salt and pepper dule,
appears throughout the cul-de-sac
with even rhythms of soft coos
and featherly caresses of smile strokes,
silver and pearl tokens on their necks
and divine libations in their hands.
Their large plumage of strong wings
maneuvers quick flight launches.

They keep predators at bay
in a constant guard of scouting rituals.

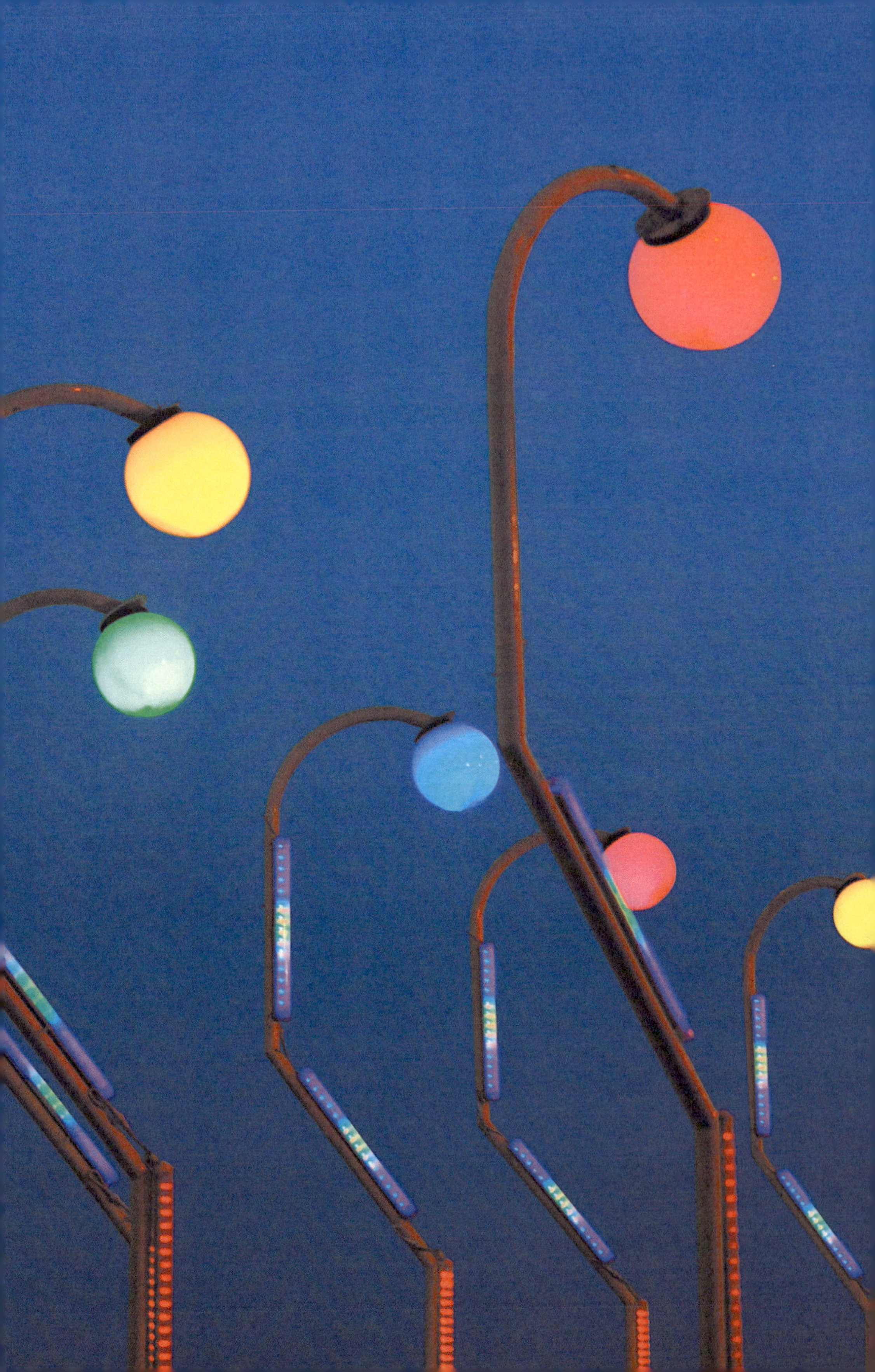

14 Brain Landscape

The labyrinth's folds
of my brain's paths and alleys
hide new mystery enhancements.
Scared and silent cerebral lesions
learn to dodge moving bullets
in a hide-&-seek cranial dance,
expecting a precious interlude of relief,
a precarious respite between songs,
the moment of resection.

Cells must mute their spread cues
at the Gamma Knife command
or await further cyber radio orders.
I give them calming French music
and sweet rainbow gummies
mixed with visions of glowing color hues.

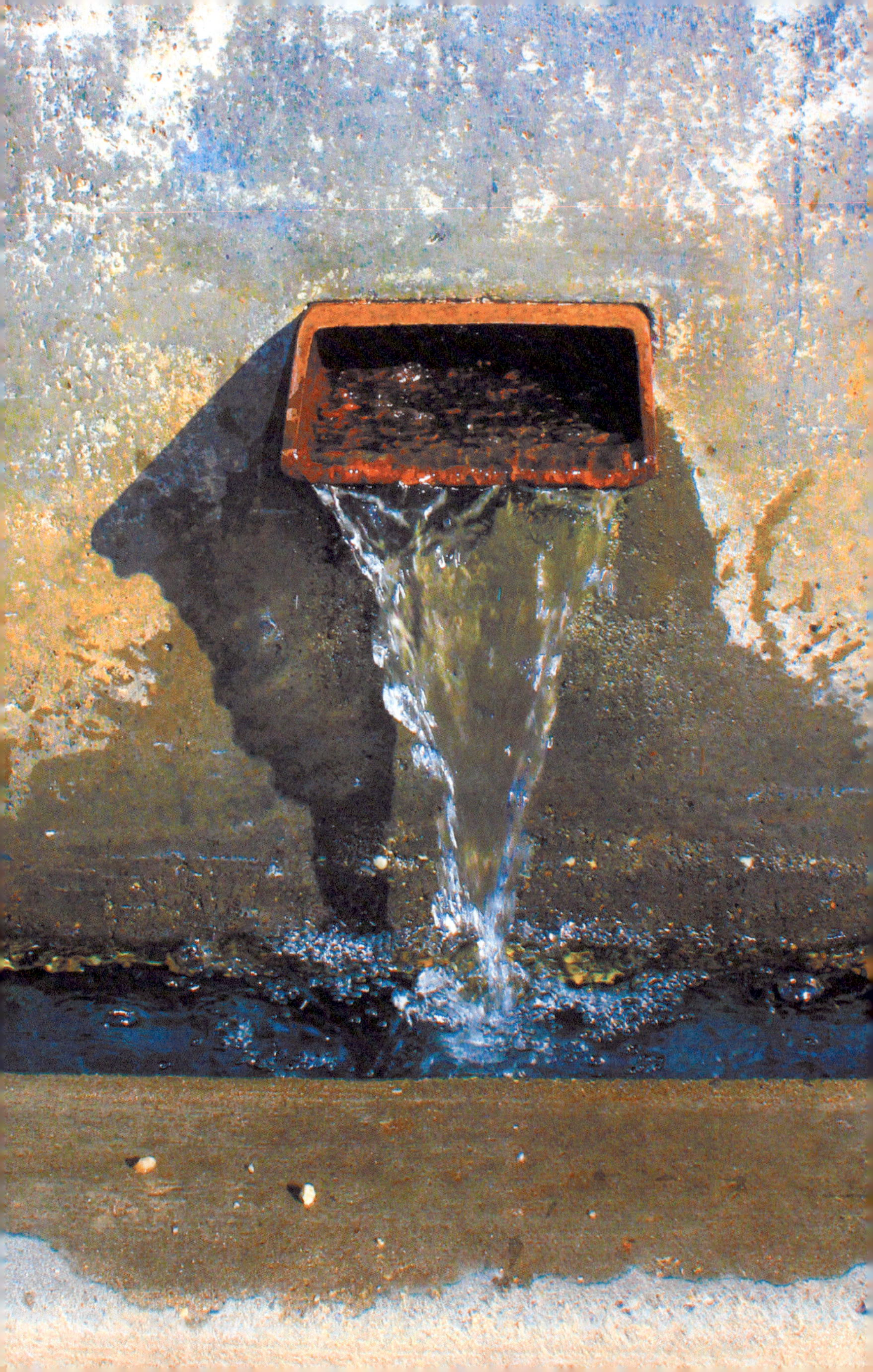

15 Wash Away

Warned be all screechy echoes
in my encircling havoc of fear:
watch for the quick sable fall
that will slice your weight in two.
We don't play shadow games
while sharpness is our weapon,
nor we ever put down war tools.
We don't rehearse fake combats
nor keep blood drops on open tombs.

Just back out and retreat silently,
we'll look away and dilute your existence.

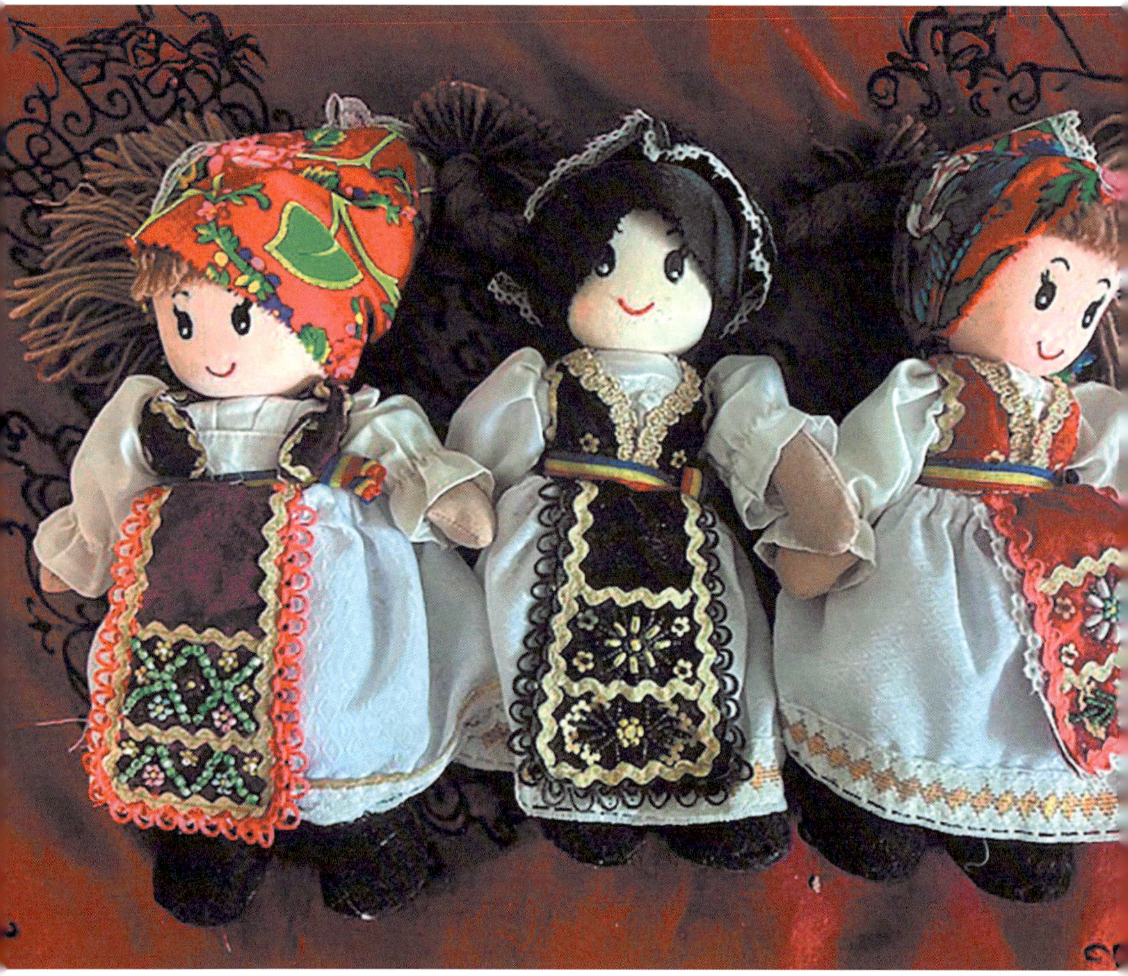

16 Hermana (*Même sans l'même sang*)

My shining sister appears, proudly, in full,
no private show hides behind her doors.
A fierce star from a Balkan constellation
of limitless whiz and human brilliance,
tinted by cosmic notes of death's ballads
with Roma flavors and eastern aromas,
held by the impetus of a bursting sun.

Casting her aura's bright velvet blanket,
she's ready to share fears and laughters,
to let me curate her tears in necklace strings,
to twist, break, snap, or remake shapes at will,
to dance and cry our pasts and our presents,
to stumble and stand in moonlight old prances,
to retrain our fate with circling suitcases.

Pulling our dreams, hands, and thoughts tight
through unrooted paths of shared earthly exiles,
we carry raw hearts between our fingers,
lost and found entrails from life's hard scuffles
to retain and rewrite and return to our essence
the calmness embrace of a long numbing holler
buried beneath the mirror of warm lithium waters.

Berry delights of ἀμβροσία await
while we blow away murky dust hurdles.
Même sans l'même sang, on s'aimera.

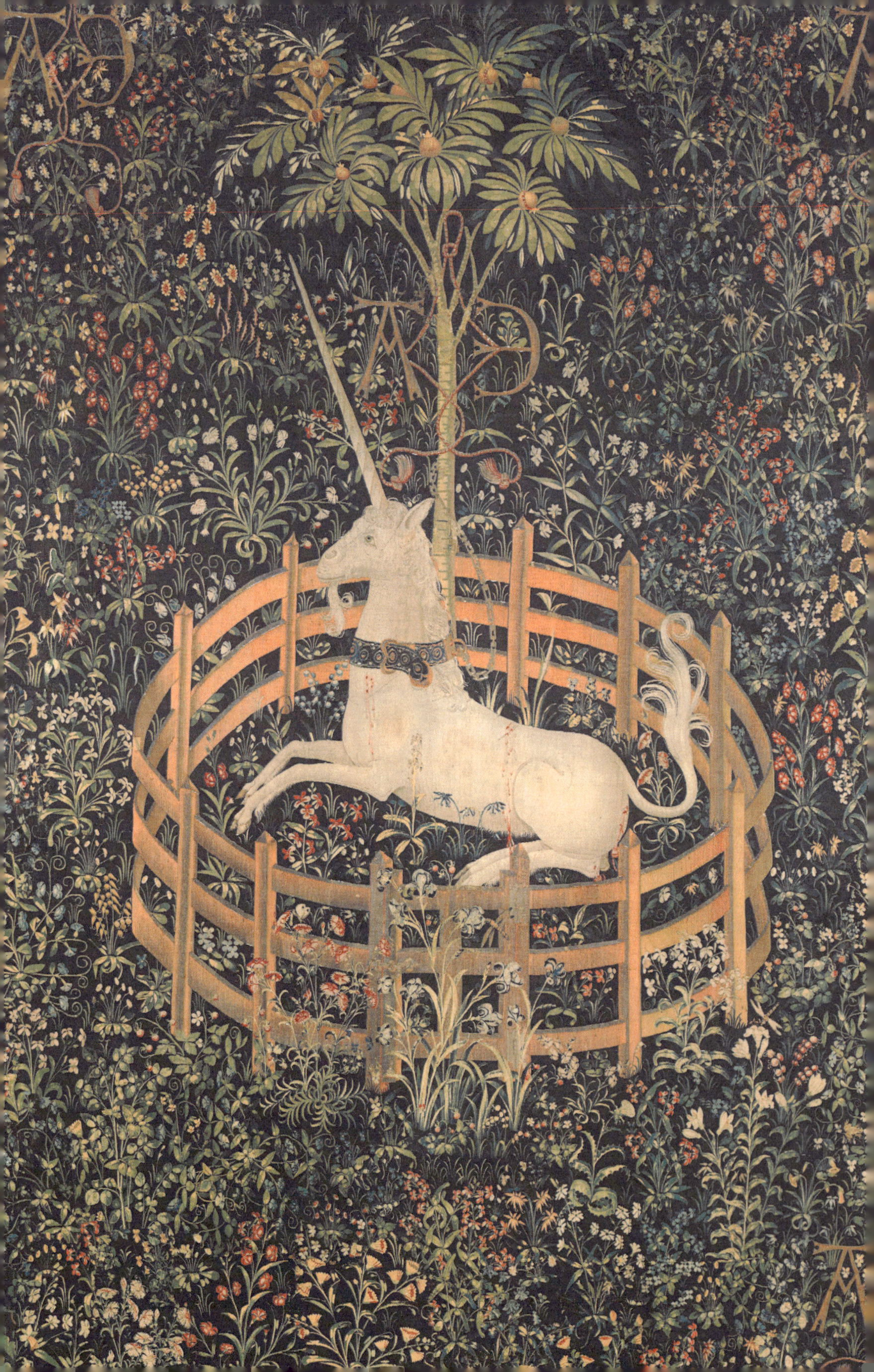

17 What it Can't

This intruder can't muffle my spirit,
spoil the serenity of my being,
or consume the fortitude of love.

Can't ravage the peace of days,
wreck the shrine of eternal life,
or quell the whims of loving memories.

It will not crush courage,
quiet the impetus of my thirst,
or decimate my mind's curiosity.

Can't extinguish my well of joy,
can't gag this heart's capricious grit,
or subdue the marvels of the mind.

It will not quash my quirks and quibbles,
smother the smoking fibers of my resolve,
or tangle the embroidery of my tapestry.

That, it can't.

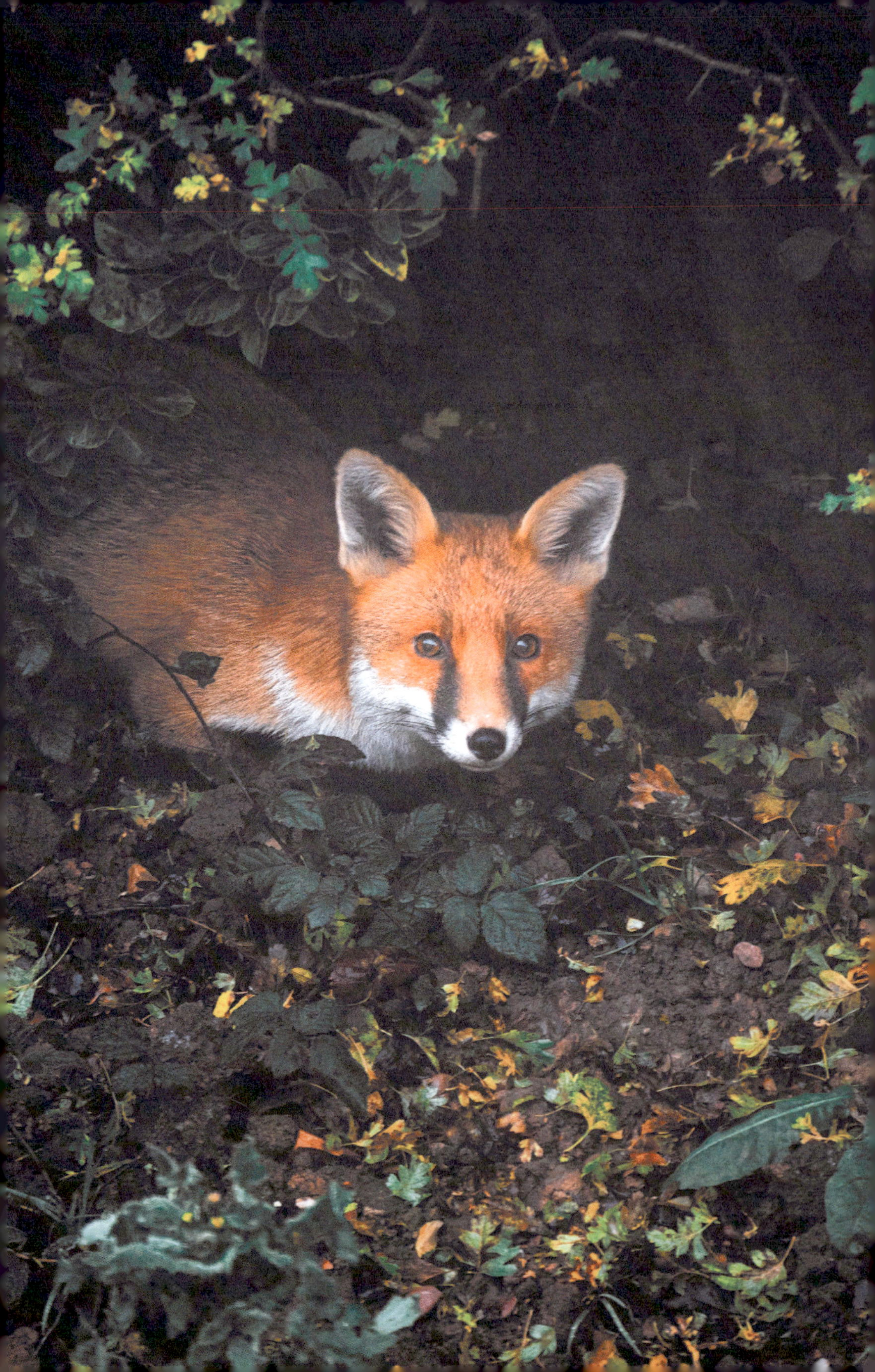

18 A Vixen's Litter of Hopes

With an elegant tread
and sly nocturnal walk
the red vixen gathers
her magnetic forces
in a ring of shadows
when rising waters
sweep her hopes away.
She finds their howling basket
by a perilous stream,
and licking their sobs
clean of muddy fears,
she nurses their might,
full of care and zeal.
In her burrow she builds
a plan to break off
the root of this storm
from her litter of hopes.

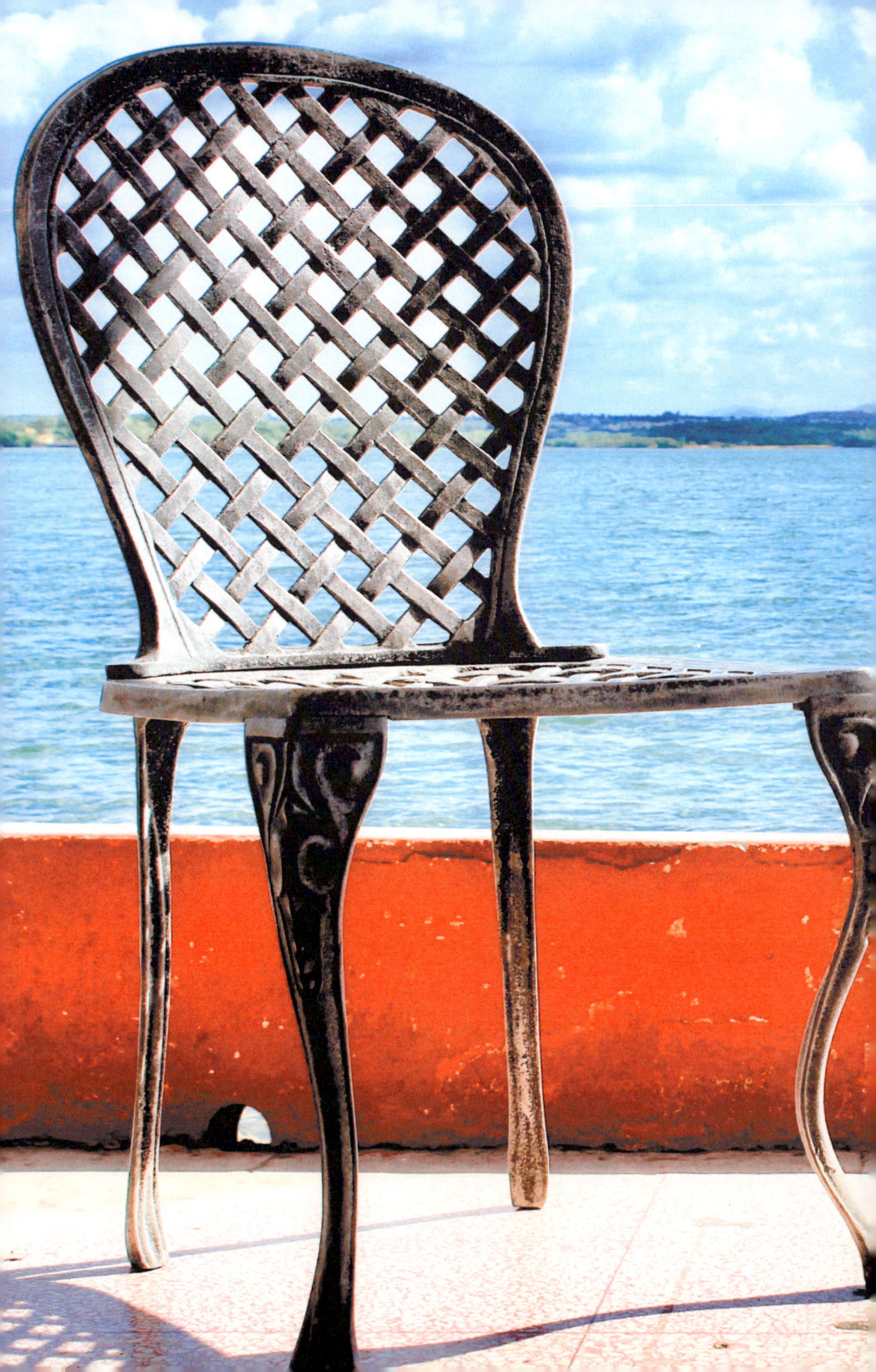

19 Across the Waiting Area

A new part of you came along today
holding you softly in that chair,
giving yourselves space to be;
bless its delicate presence.
May it walk you slowly through the day
moving in unison with your rhythm.
This part of the self does not give up,
it has dared to prop a luminous you,
to unfold your solemn power,
your essence, with its presence.
May you smile at its inner grace,
delve into its reflection,
seek its tender depths
while its soft touch holds you warmly.
Praise it, praise you.
May it charge your gentle light
with a serene new luster.
Listen and trust its worth
with a brave caring thought:
YOU matter.
The universe is making way.

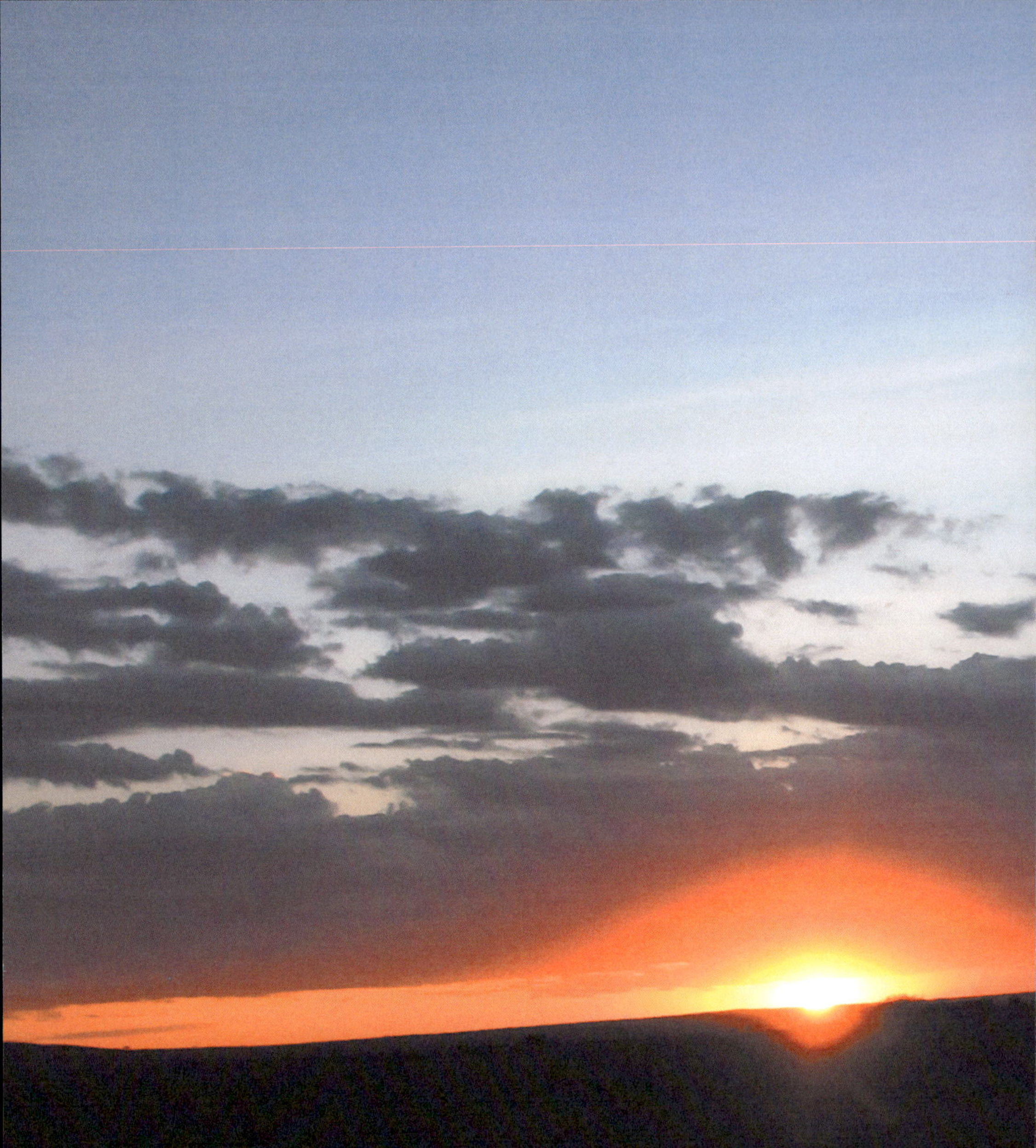

20 Finitude

I ascend my quivering finitude
but the whirl to believe gulps me
and I watch turmoils drift away
while inhaling lavender scents.

I endure each lingering new peak
from a precipice thrashing at my feet
and sustain myself on a promise pebble
that's not eroded by the fear of dimness.

As I climb this bleak life pinnacle
I gather the words I left behind
to write away grief and pain
and weave peace into my soul's fibers.

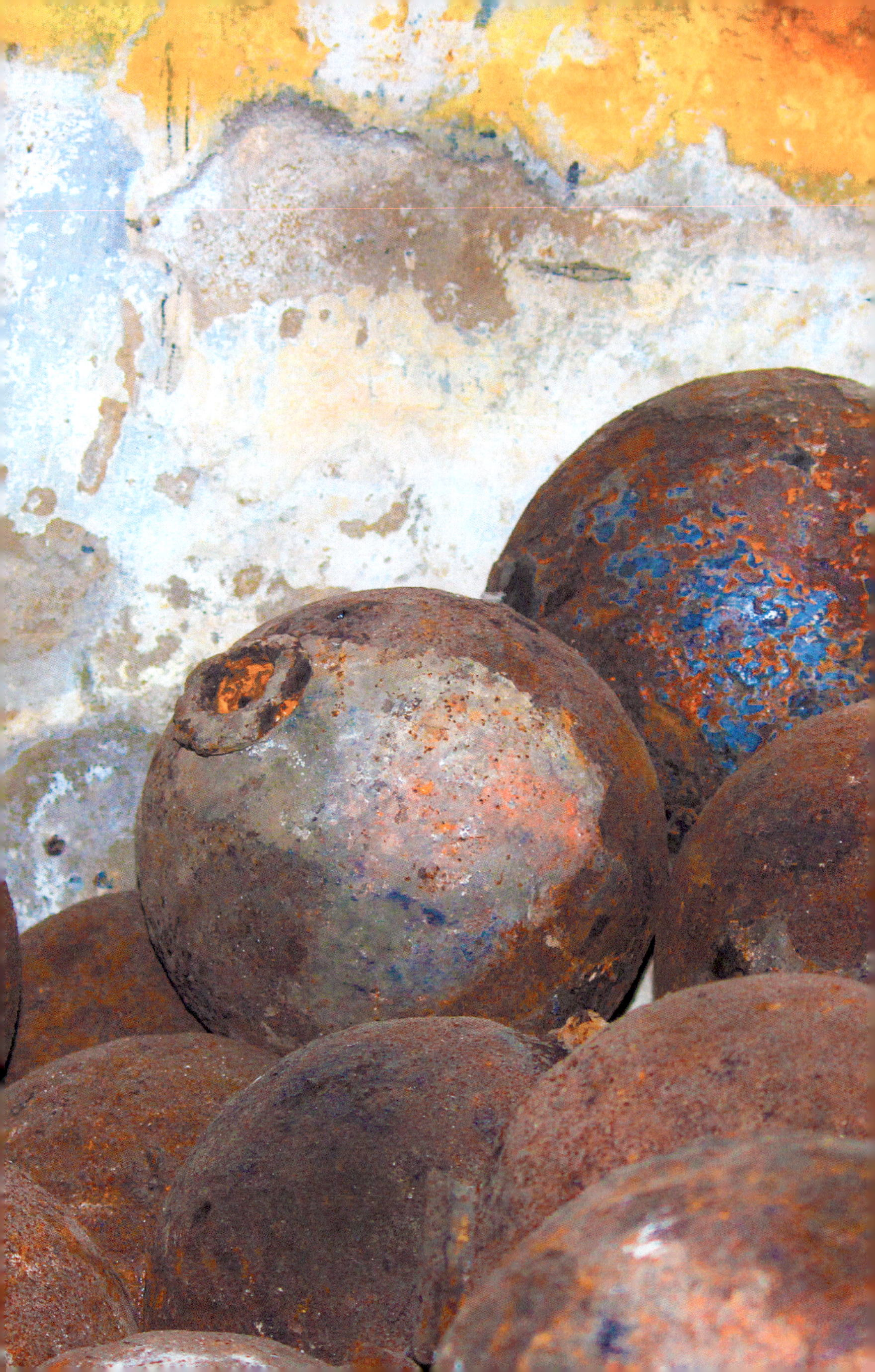

21 Cannon Balls or Butterflies

No need to decipher enchained codes,
places where the mind has never trod,
toil only in a netherworld of unchained matter.
Don't send cannon balls to souls' gates,
lace only live nerve ends to escape chaos,
and pluck those who never truly were.
Hold only onto a heart's presence
and just deliver the old fable:
one coherent enough to yield sound life nets,
to unearth the root of a divine talisman,
to uncover the tropes in the ropes,
and scrape any muted dull clutter.
Ignore the shrieking echoes of disturbing ilks,
never sit there aghast and deafened.
Drop those who await your death
as the perfect excuse to greet you.

I'll write the last scenes of my story's finale,
when the main cast and background orchestra
let loose in frothing chants of pure animal joy.
Then, I'll go to the edge of the light,
where butterflies flutter on the wings of my thoughts.

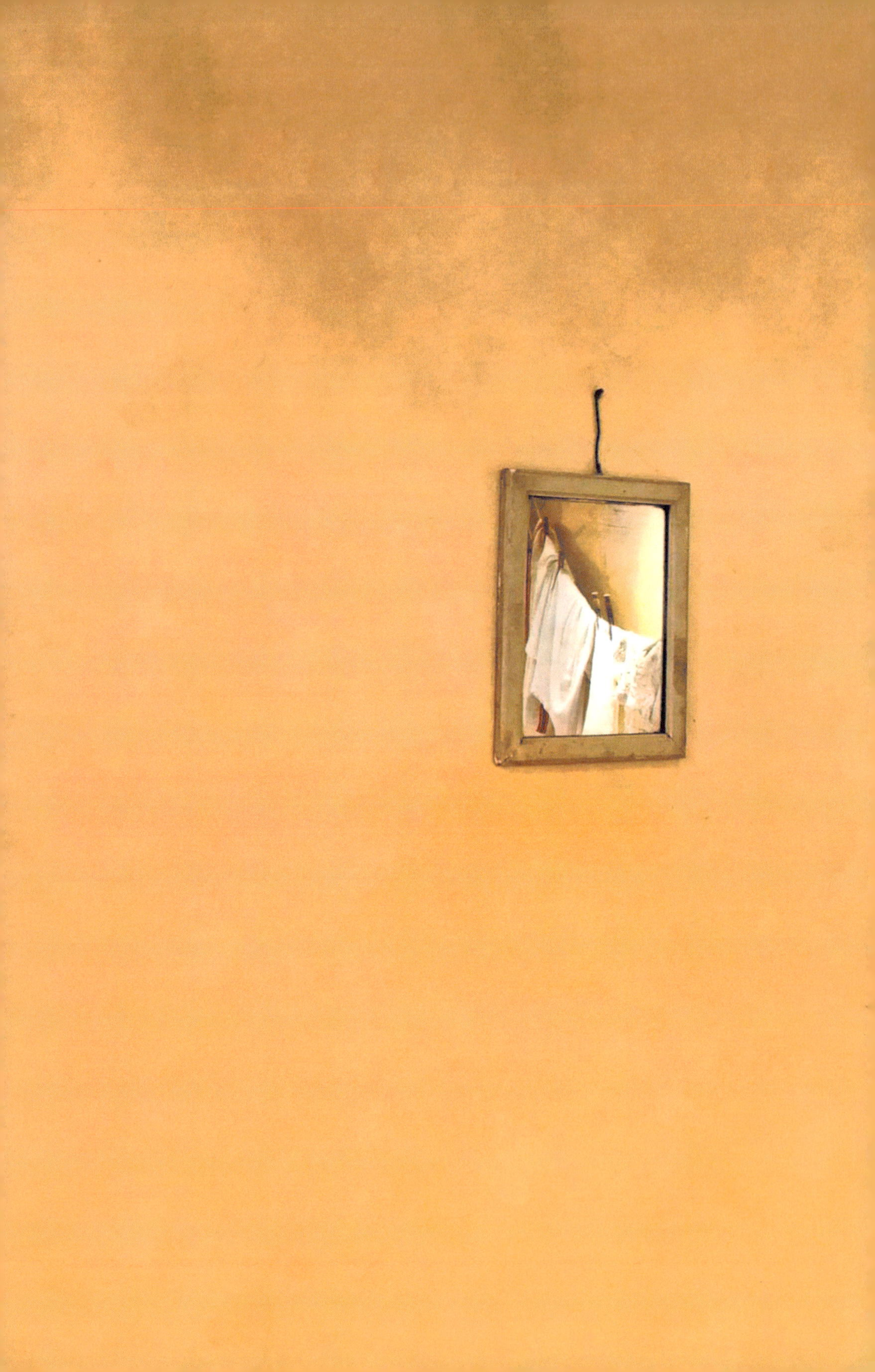

22 Mirror

The locks left her mirror.
Their texture, their color,
so uselessly mattered,
so vainly she fret about them.
She hated and tamed
her bouncy brown curls,
with highlights, with irons,
with dyes, and with pins.

Each falling strand
stabbed her pride and calm.
So fruitless her efforts,
so barren the endeavors.
Each loss brought a heartbreak,
more anguish to top her struggle
till their absence screamed
and shattered her mirror
while blasting her woes:

your dearth is an infant,
your bareness is life,
your hope is not empty
you're here, you're alive.

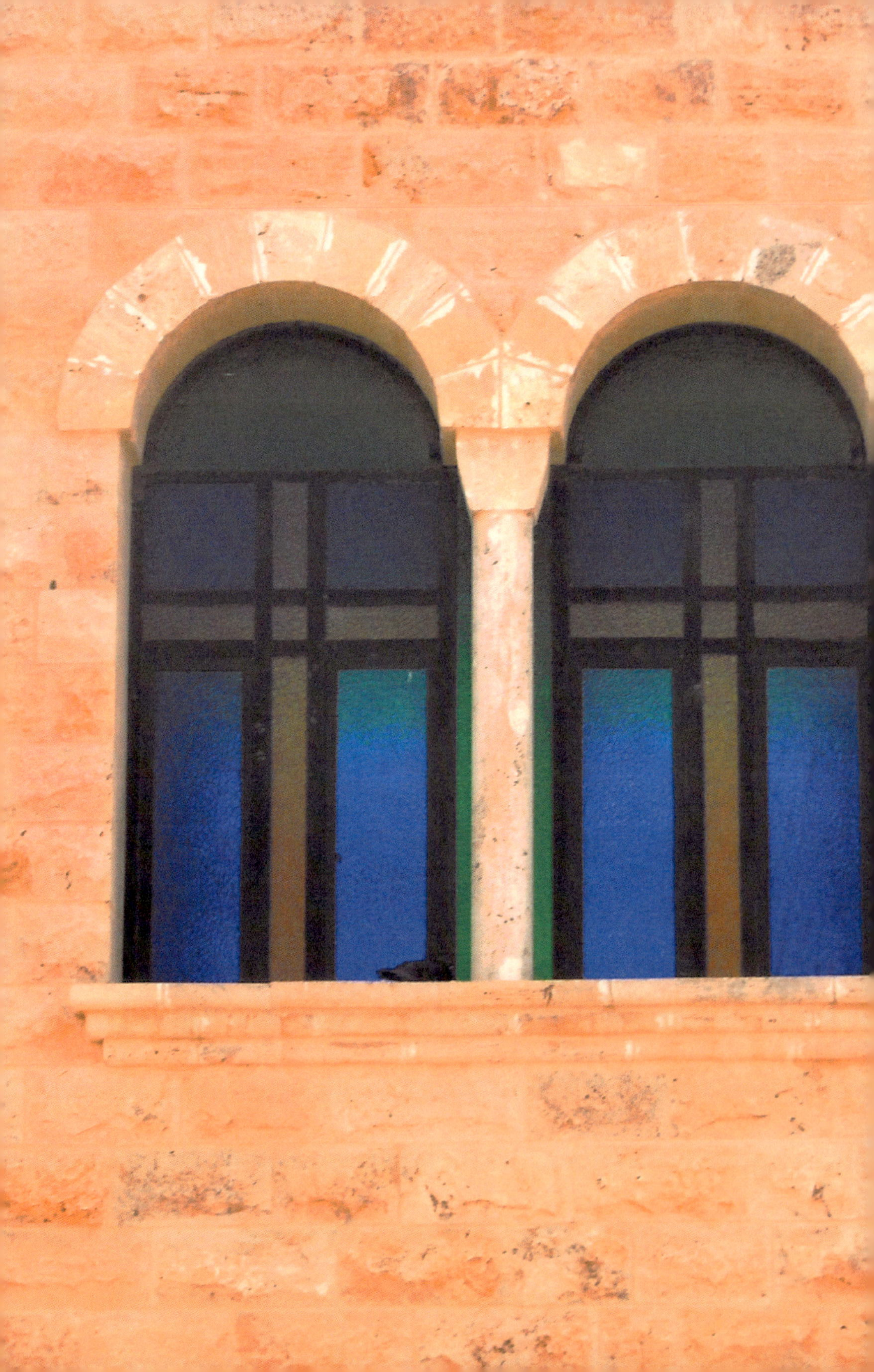

23 My Two Souls

'Desinunt ista, non pereunt.'
(Seneca the Younger, *Ad Lucilium Epistulae Morales.* XXXVI.)

When you wake up
And I am not there,
You must believe
I live in you.

Your souls are filled
With my old gaze,
My soft caress,
My eternal joy of you.

Your skin is layered
With all my hugs,
With all the kisses
I engraved in you.

If one day reason
Denies I am near,
Through each step,
Through every turn,
You'll find a clue
and it'll be clear:
An eternal star,
A word, a hue,
A glare, a flare,
A look, a root,
A bead, a stone,
A trace of scent,
A little tune.

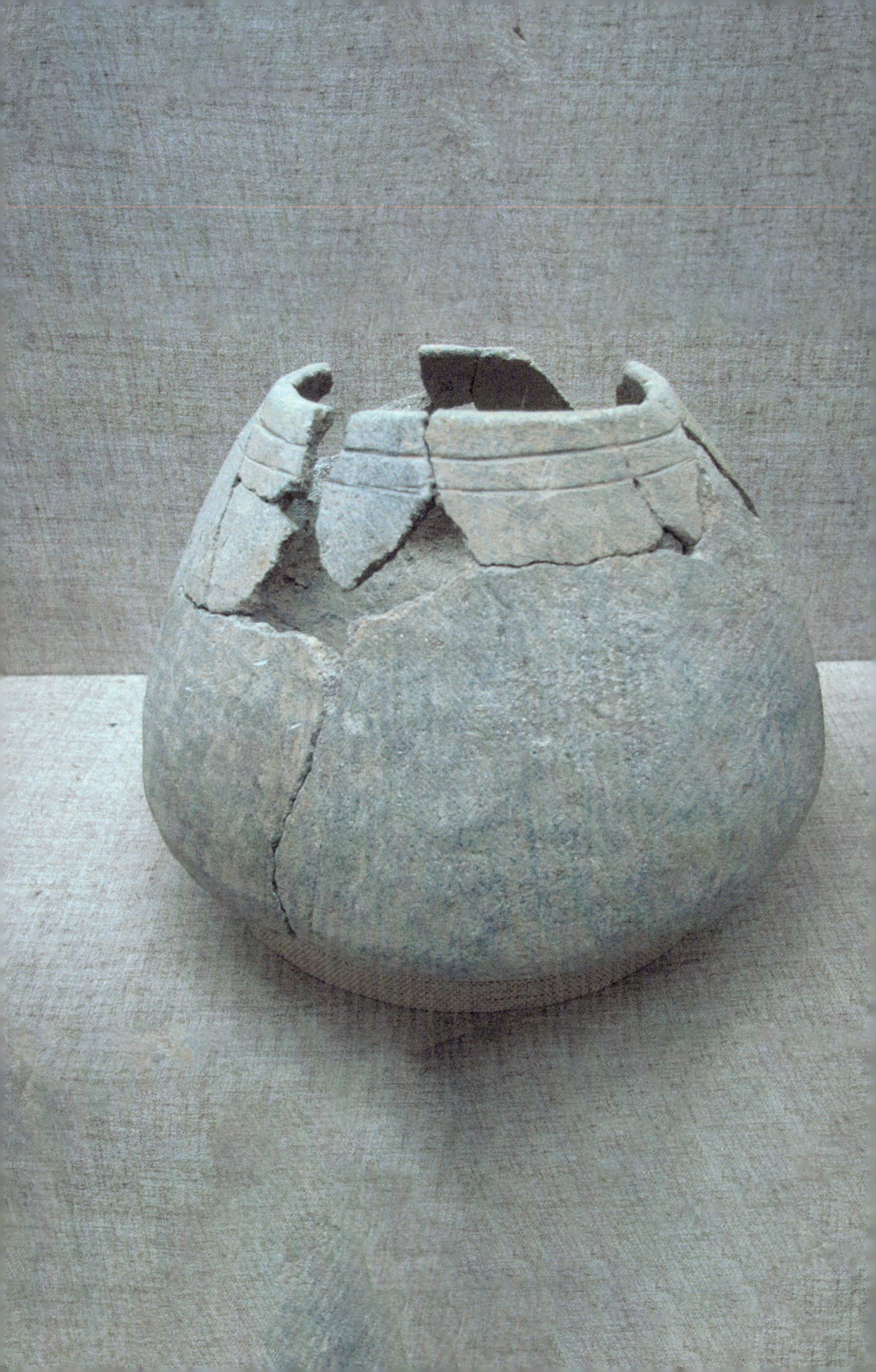

24 Shards

Shards of fear are shattered at my feet.
From above I can hardly distinguish
my old splintered reflections,
deflections of bright selves, and young rays,
sound once, speckless once.

A questing mind, a prying curiosity
urges me to pick one up.
A distorted resemblance of me stares
begging to lash out from the ground,
to join in despair a phantom whole.
Frantic reflections glance at my eyes
through crystalline slivers
and bright sharp edges,
each flashing fading memories
to blanket their rusty angst with new shine.

The brittle sliver I grab slashes my fingers,
and the sharpness of the cut stings.
Blood runs from thumb to elbow
dripping smothering drops of anger ghosts,
old stain reminders from a late me.
The veins are too close ...
yet the mind watches closer:
Drop it, shed that shard!
Open your palm and let go!
Never dare to touch a single flake!

Dance on them instead,
Jump, stamp, thump with your soles,
follow the beat with a tireless throb.
Crush them, smash them with your heels
till they turn into sand,
till jagged edges are pulverized once and for all,
too little to pierce, unable to splint,
handfuls of powerless dust impotent to harm,
to scatter into the sea, fated to sink,
attached to crusty treasures and an ocean of sins.

Brush leftover glitter from your fingers!
Blow away all barren smithereens at last!

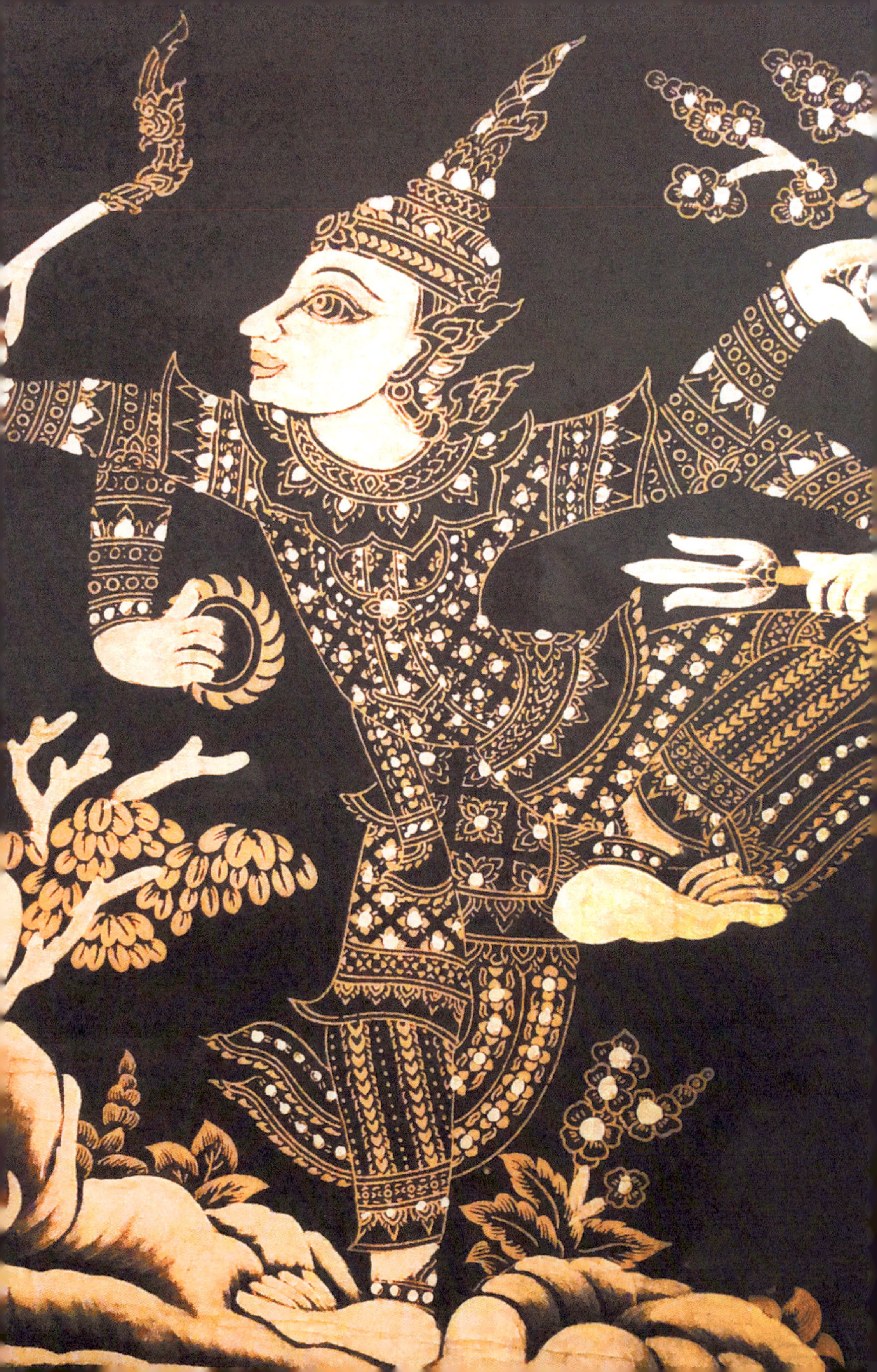

25 All Over Again

Make a fist
it'll hurt a bit
drink the whole cup
here's a warm blanket
arms behind your head
any music preferences?
another warm blanket?
we'll need a new IV spot
here comes the contrast
hold still and don't move
not claustrophobic, right?
squeeze if you need us to stop
hold your breath ... breathe now

Low platelets
stand on the scale
we'll flush your port
nausea, nausea, nausea
someone plays a calming piano
we'll see you again in a couple of weeks
more stabs, more sticks, more scans, more ...

Will I ever ring the bell?

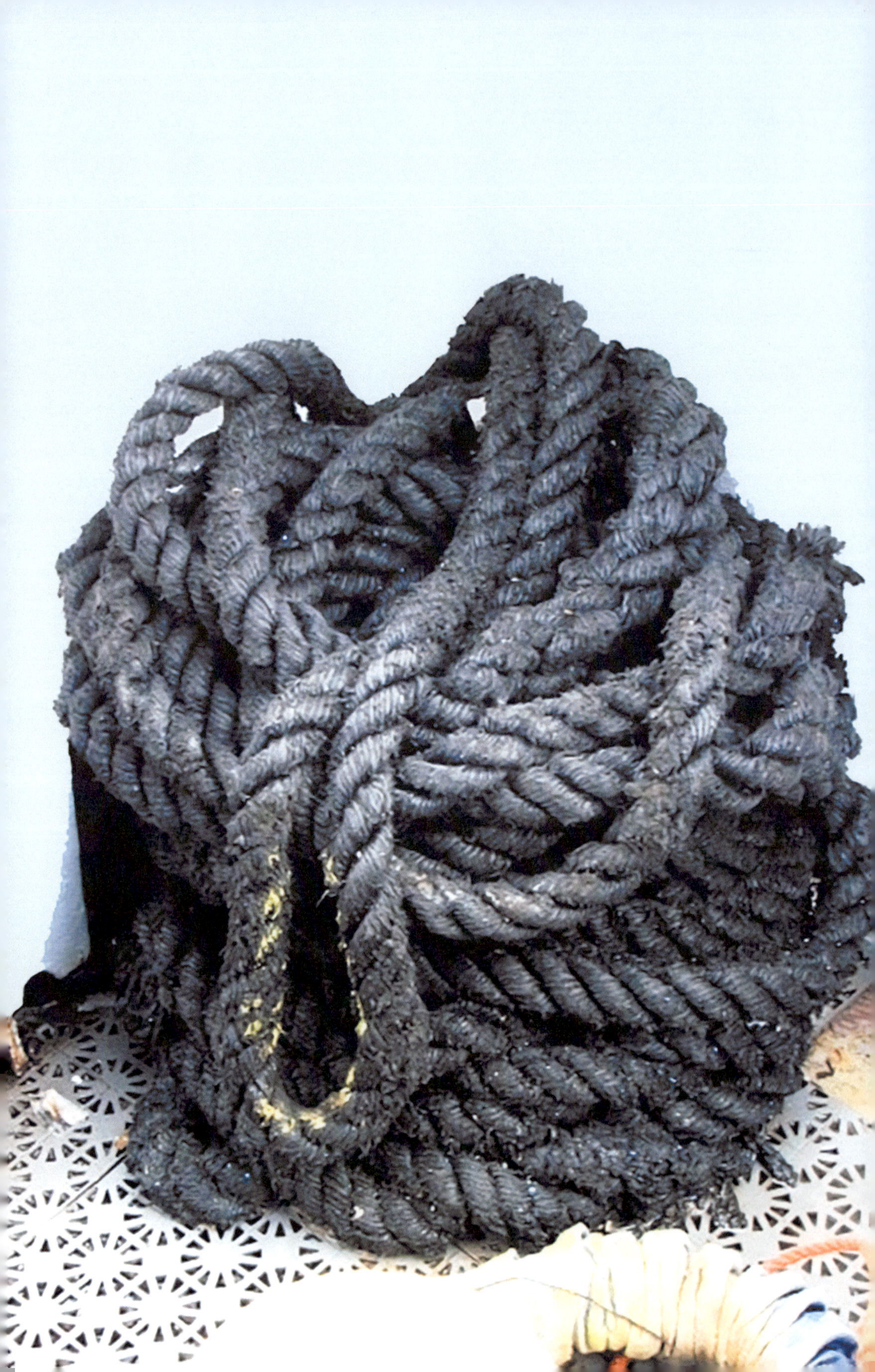

26 Ariadne

Looming pain and fear
have twisted old fibers
in your body with the knots
of an entangled jute rope.
You have collapsed
into a trembling heap,
an old ball laying there
disheveled on the ground,
limp and thwarted.

But Ariadne inhabits you
to unbind, to untie,
to unravel without scissors,
to weave out frightened strands,
to unfurl the coarse yarn,
to knit a soft silk ribbon,
and glide out of the maze
into a newly braided world.
Dionysus will join you at Naxos.

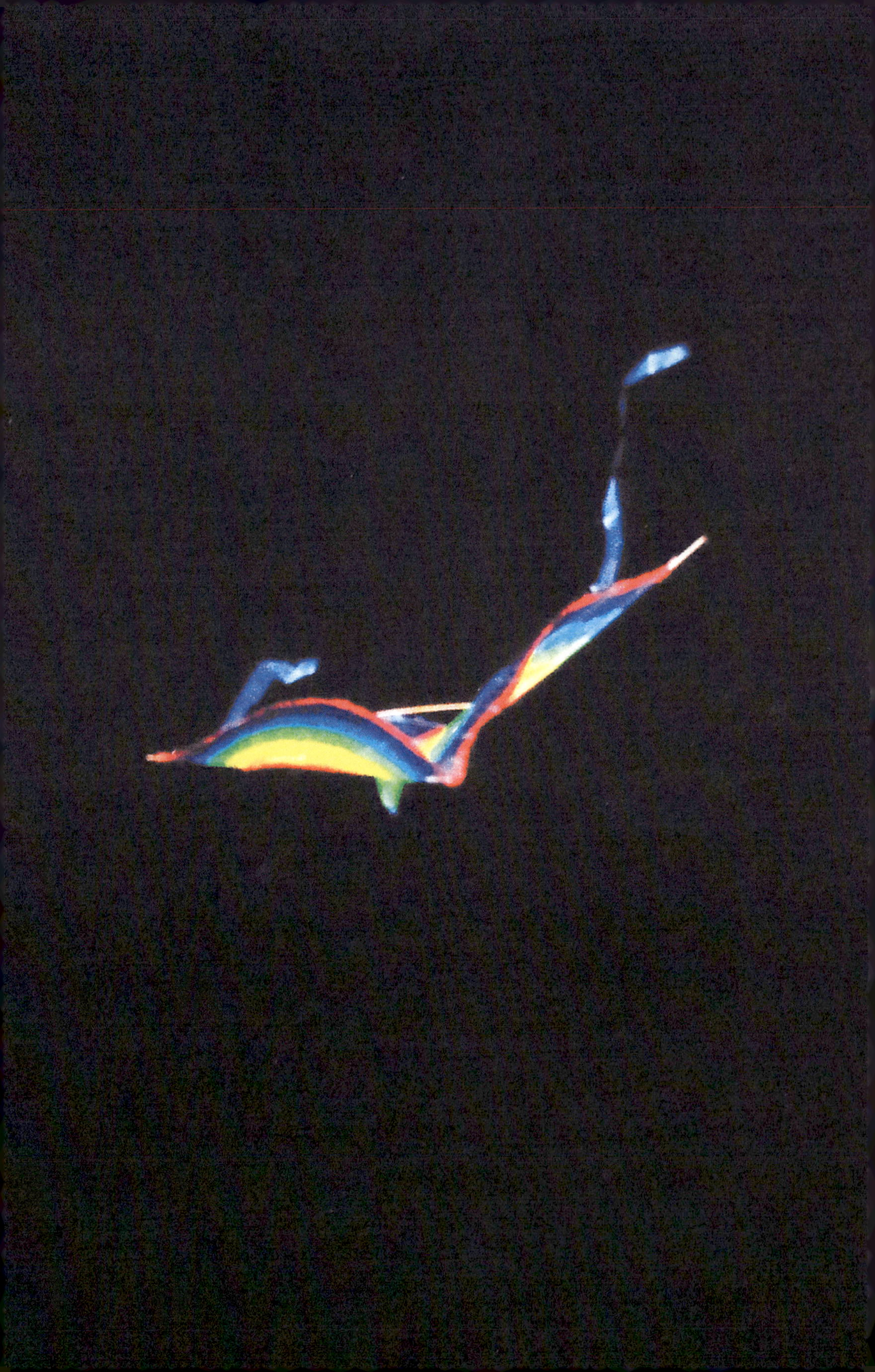

27 Step Out & Repeat

Step out of your former self
observe the fabric of YOU
gently peel away the unreal
watch your glorious essence
always there, always present
harness your magic
clap your iridescent wings
and regale your person
with gifts for the now
take a fluttery detour
before returning inside
embrace your damsel power
laugh at your own quirks
embolden your crazy
blend a smile into your mirror
at the start of each day
and truly see you
make a batch of self-love
reset your rhythm
resow, resew, renew
rest and restore
redirect your flight
relish the moment
redraw your dreams
remain alert.
Repeat.

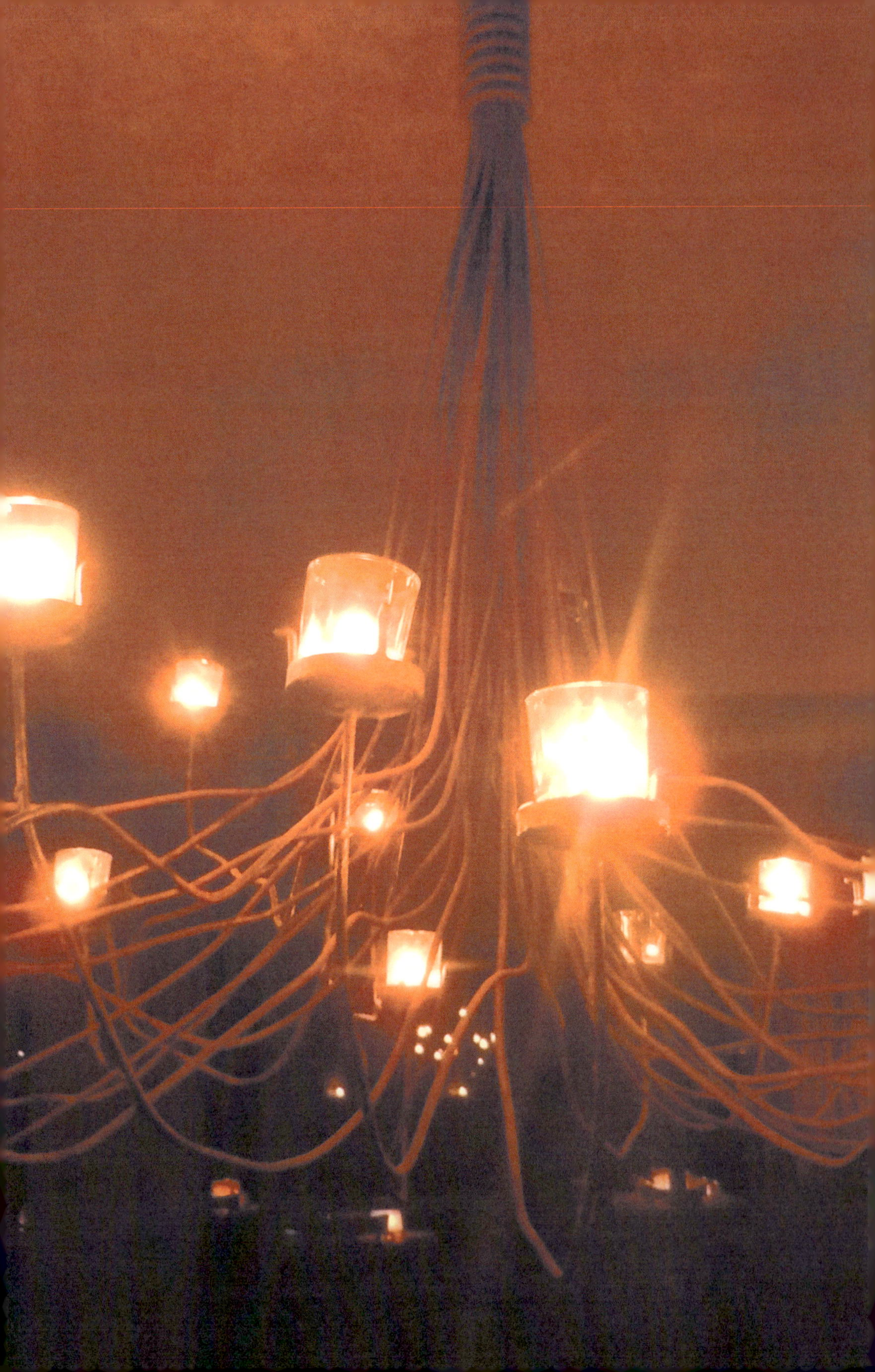

28 Prayers

Prayers taunt me, knock at the door, offer themselves to me.
Some tease me into trusting their God's miraculous Male hand.
Mine summon the universe's power and my own strength.

Long gone are the 'holy' messages I learned as a child.
I dutifully tried to memorize a plethora of *orations*
for the Catholic God or His pantheon's deified servants:
strings of fancy words and vague sentences,
recited under naive fears of divine reprimands
or extended kneeling time when forgetting the words.
No, one could never remember everything,
the exact words to fit specific occasions and spaces,
saints, martyrs, deities, and their blessings,
the commas, the pauses, the rhythms, the gestures,
standing, kneeling, eyes closed, eyes opened,
hands folded, hands upraised, holding hands with others,
head up, head down, a holy cross drawn from head to chest …
unless maybe a melody came to offer some rescue.
I was told that '*rezar oraciones*' was far more pious
than daringly '*pedir*' specifics from sacrosanct beings:
"They know what you need already, use the right words!"
I needed to appeal without asking, suggest without saying,
and, most of all, plead to convince without begging.

The practice contradicted alternative innocent choices,
and searches for true meanings were penalized or derided.
Spontaneous creative sentences from a forgetful girl,
crafted in despair or in fear of a nun's punishment,
moments of surrender to intentional communication,
true invocation, a supplication for intercession,
a cry for help instead of memorized saintly prayers,
all pulverized.

West of the Atlantic, I discovered expanded prayers.
Those had merged, adapted, and some even blossomed.
Offers of prayers or a place in someone's prayers,
are given often, announced, claimed, and even gifted.
I welcome them and that should be it. Period. I know.
I'm grateful, blessed. I feel loved and cared for.
But my inquisitive mind still seeks to understand:

are they prayers or petitions? hopes or wishes? to whom?
about what? about my body? about my future?
to undo and reverse what has been done so far?
about my soul? to bless and cleanse a cursed part of me?
to commend me further to their God? to offer consolation?
to bring a little less pain hereafter? to actually cure and heal?
to correct a doomed divine path?
Wait, was a mistake made along the way?
Was there a fatal flaw God was unaware of?

Can we, through prayers, reach God's past or present?
His future purpose to make Him change His mind?
His future will? His past actions? His current plans?
His attention to humanity?
Did He ask for this?
If not, what things do prayers achieve?
They mold our accepting submission to God's will,
even when it inexorably kills our bodies?

I am still lost in the prayer labyrinth.
Is that one of the reasons for limbo's internment?
An indefinite purgatory sentence?

www.ingramcontent.com/pod-product-compliance
Ingram Content Group UK Ltd.
Pitfield, Milton Keynes, MK11 3LW, UK
UKRC031052310726
14090UKWH00028B/480

* 9 7 8 1 9 1 0 1 4 6 9 4 1 *

9 781910 146941